SPEAKEASY

Lynn Aliya

SPEAKEASY

A Radically New Approach to Public Speaking

(Less Fear, More Fun)

Illustrations by Tonia Jenny

Barrow Street

Printed in the United States of America

First Printing, 2024

ISBN-13: 979-8-9910435-5-7 (Paperback edition)

Editor, Designer, Illustrator: Tonia Jenny www.toniajenny.com

Published by Lynn Aliya

speakeasymethod@gmail.com

www.speakeasymethod.net

To Kai and Jaymin, the voices of the future.

Contents

According to most studies, people's number one fear is public speaking. Number two is death. Death is number two. Does that sound right? This means to the average person, if you go to a funeral, you're better off in the casket than doing the eulogy.

—Jerry Seinfeld

Preface

Do you remember when you were a kid playing games like Mad Libs or paint-by-numbers? They were partially composed stories or pictures where you simply fill in the blanks, and *voilà!* With each stroke of color or verb ending in '-ing,' your creation came to life.

These games were so rewarding because they always worked out; all you needed to do was follow the template. I'd always wished there was a customized template for public speaking or a game with a pre-written speech where I could just insert a funny adjective, an article of clothing or a body part, and presto, my presentation was done!

Much to my dismay (and surprise), no such resource existed. So, I created one. Introducing a template-esque method for public speaking. This book will guide you through a process, from writing your speech to presenting. The whole shebang, from page to stage—the SPEAKEASY Method™—simplifies your speech-writing process, fosters creativity and bolsters your confidence when delivering any kind of presentation.

The SPEAKEASY Method™ will radically change the way you approach and prepare for public speaking engagements (or any type of presentation) by providing you with the necessary tools to increase your confidence, significantly reduce anxiety, alleviate the fear of criticism and self-judgment, help lower your heart rate and communicate easily that which you truly hope to share.

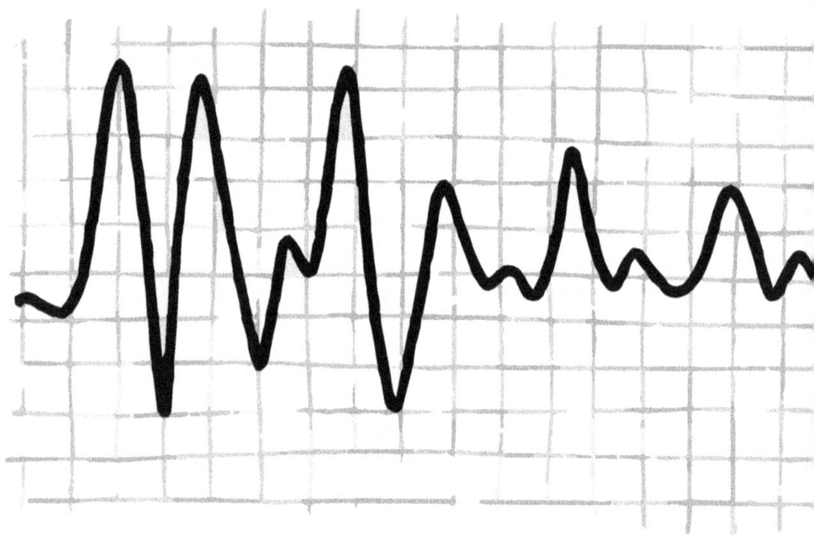

You're about to experience an unconventional, out-of-the-box approach to public speaking. I'm asking you to set aside your skepticism and logical reasoning. Forget everything you've learned about public speaking before. (Because, let's face it, where has that gotten you? It's gotten you fear, worry and now to this book, which is exactly where you need to be.)

The SPEAKEASY Method™ disrupts your linear thought patterns by venturing beyond traditional step-by-step logic, challenging everything you've learned about speaking in public.

Public speaking is not natural. Yet, we're expected to speak naturally in public. Actors and performers undergo extensive training for this skill. They rehearse, attend schools, and work with directors to appear natural. This technique will immerse you in that mindset.

Memorization is terrifying for most of us, but in real life, when you speak in front of an audience, you'll never need to memorize anything after junior high school. You will never be asked to stand before a group without notes or prompts. You will not be given demerits if you use your hands to articulate your ideas, nor will you be criticized for pausing to gather your thoughts.

SPEAKEASY isn't about memorization. It is about moving past everything you've been taught before about public speaking, letting go of your own expectations of what you think you should sound and look like, and learning to trust your own wisdom and authentic voice.

I've spent three decades in the entertainment industry as a radio broadcaster, award-winning actor, communications professor and public speaking coach. In this book, I will share the strategies I've learned. You'll see what makes for a dynamic speech, setting clear objectives and actions.

You'll also learn proven principles from performance experts; the greatest secrets of theatre, film and improvisation; harnessing the superpower of emojis, all of which provide tools and tips to build confidence and skill.

SPEAKEASY is sophisticated enough for the most experienced senior spokesperson and approachable enough for novice speakers just starting their journey, including people who don't like public speaking. By the end of this book, you'll be eager to present in front of an audience, pitch ideas confidently or deliver that memorable wedding toast.

Regardless of your age or level of experience, SPEAKEASY taps into your own ingenuity by providing a platform and structure to equip you to articulate your ideas and convey them with intelligence, power and courage.

Intelligence
Power
Courage
YOUR
INGENUITY

Introduction

Legend has it that Dr. Martin Luther King Jr., one of the greatest orators in history, received a "C" in a college public speaking course. Similarly, exceptional communicators like Oprah Winfrey and Steve Jobs faced their own hurdles. Oprah was harshly judged for her speaking style, even being labeled "unfit for television" in her first job. Likewise, Jobs was criticized for failing to make his jargon-heavy presentations understandable.

I hear you; you're thinking, *I'm not Oprah or MLK, I just need to get through this presentation without fainting.* You've likely picked up this book because you're facing your own speaking challenges. Whether it's delivering a wedding toast, presenting at a professional conference or addressing the city council, the idea of public speaking can leave you feeling stranded and overwhelmed, thinking, *I just need a quick fix. What the heck do I do right now? I hate speaking in public.*

Feeling this way is understandable and reminiscent of George Spelvin's predicament in the comic play "The Actor's Nightmare." Spelvin, an accountant, finds himself mistakenly cast as an actor and thrust onto the stage without any rehearsal. Chaos ensues as he struggles with anxiety, speaks in gibberish and grapples with stage directions, resulting in a disastrous performance.

This mirrors the anxiety many of us feel when asked to speak in public. Regardless of our backgrounds, it can feel like a life-and-death situation, akin to embarking on a wilderness expedition without a compass.

To navigate this anxiety, it's good to recognize that public speaking requires us to play multiple roles at once—content creator, stage presenter, performer, stage manager, technician, director, and subject expert. The pressure to excel in each role, especially without proper training or guidance, is frightening.

What's the secret then to public speaking?

If you only learn one thing from this entire book or don't read past this paragraph, make it this: stop dwelling on yourself and focus the spotlight where it belongs—on your audience.

Making your audience your number one priority automatically shifts your attention off yourself and onto them. It's like an automatic pressure-release valve, instantly reducing the stress and anxiety of public speaking. Your number one goal is to connect and share ideas with your listeners. The key to any great performance is making your audience the focus, not yourself. When you shine the spotlight on them, you find the true magic of connection.

Your number one task as a speaker is to build an idea inside the minds of your audience.
— Chris Anderson, Curator of TED Talks

Forget everything you have
learned about public speaking
Lynn Aliya
SPEAKEASY
LESS FEAR
MORE FUN
A Radically New Approach
to Public Speaking
Aliya
SPEAKEASY
86

How to Use This Book

Just like following a recipe, to get the most out of this book, I recommend following its structured approach and clear steps. The SPEAKEASY Method™ is deliberately designed to free you from blank-page syndrome and the pressure of perfection, allowing your creativity to flow uninterrupted. Much like assembling IKEA furniture, it may seem daunting at first glance. However, as you start to piece together what you learn, step by step, it will come together with ease.

After "The Basics" section, each of the three parts in this book offer practical strategies and techniques to improve your communication skills, connect meaningfully with your audience and boost your innovative ideas.

- **Part One:** You'll quickly write your script using the SPEAKEASY Method™. This process captures your scattered thoughts and ideas, gathers them together, arranges them in a successful sequence, and *automagically* transfers them onto paper, providing a framework for your speech.
- **Part Two**: This section delves into dissecting and refining your script, beginning with distilling Your Mission. You'll break down your script to identify your objectives—desires, actions, and tactics—to get what you want from and for your audience.
- **Part Three**: You'll learn rehearsal techniques that take you from page to stage, creating a comprehensive plan for in-person or virtual presentations. You'll start with blocking (ways to map out your movements), running a tech rehearsal, getting valuable feedback and preparing for Murphy's Law. By the end of this part, you'll be eager and confident to step into the spotlight, knowing 'you got this.'

If you get the basics right everything else falls into place.

—Lewis Pugh

The Basics

(Tenets of the SPEAKEASY Method™)

Before diving into the fun of crafting your speech, there are a few foundational concepts I'd like you to keep in mind as you go about the process of creating and refining what it is you will ultimately be sharing with others.

The Audience

Your relationship with your audience is like falling in love: You're giddy, nervous and flushed, with your heart pounding in anticipation. You feel faint and want to tell them everything all at once. You hear a voice in your head saying, "Slow it down," but you can't. Just as in any harmonious relationship, where both parties must actively participate to keep the connection alive, engaging with your audience requires mutual effort and understanding.

Much like the dynamics of a relationship, wondering who bears responsibility when a presentation or talk falls flat, is like asking what happens when a romance loses its luster. Is it the audience's fault for not paying attention or the speaker's fault for not being engaging enough? The answer is subjective, and miscommunications can arise on both sides.

Speakers might blame their audience for being unreceptive or not listening, similar to the way partners in a relationship may fault each other for misunderstandings. Conversely, audience members may perceive the speaker as uninteresting.

Let's face it: as the speaker, it's your responsibility to keep your audience engaged. If they're bored, it's your job to fix that. Remember, in any relationship, you are always responsible for your part.

Audiences expect speakers to stay on point. They are acutely aware of the time-frame and want assurance that you won't stray off-topic. This means sticking to your allotted time, bringing something fresh to the discussion, and being organized and engaging.

Listeners have an internal clock that signals when your time is up. If you exceed your time limit, they may shift in their seats, check their phones, or turn off their video if you're on a Zoom call. These are all signs that you've lost their attention. If you notice they are becoming disengaged, it's important to figure out why, pivot, and know how to change it by asking for constructive feedback.

Don't worry; we will cover feedback in detail in Part 3.

Fear

At its core, your fear of public speaking probably lies in the dread of sounding unprofessional—maybe even like a babbling fool—or appearing incompetent in someone else's eyes. We often gauge our success by our perception of other people's opinions.

But here's the truth: Your primary goal as a public speaker is not to prove your worth. Rather, it is to convey to your audience an inspiring message that you intimately understand and care about.

Chris Anderson, founder of TED TALKS, defines successful communication as the ability to capture an audience's attention and make a lasting impact on their hearts and minds. Anderson compares this process to planting seeds in the fertile soil of the audience's minds, allowing ideas to take root and flourish.

Whether addressing a CEO, pitching a product, or delivering a eulogy or wedding toast, your objective remains the same: sharing your ideas with intention and letting those ideas expand in the minds of your listeners.

It's important to recognize that slips and mistakes will occur—whether due to nerves, a momentary memory lapse, or distraction. Many of us feel self-conscious for various reasons, such as speaking with an accent, fearing we are terrible, disliking having the spotlight on us or being shy. Some of us have been taught that using our hands is wrong and worry about what to do with them. These mishaps or quirks do not define your success. You are not an impostor. Embrace your quirks and gestures as they contribute to your distinctiveness.

Rather than worrying about what other people think or trying to impress them, here's the secret: I promise it works every time. Instead of focusing on yourself, shift your focus onto your audience. When you do this, anxiety diminishes, and you'll be happily surprised with the fun and satisfaction that takes its place.

Be a Big, Bad Actor

Being a big, bad actor means releasing the enormous pressure many people put on themselves to excel or achieve perfection. It's a philosophy that allows space and the freedom to let yourself off the hook. Give yourself permission to move past the need for greatness or how you think greatness should look and sound. True greatness comes from your ability to share your ideas freely.

We're learning how to communicate, which is very different from concerning ourselves with superficialities. We are not all seasoned professionals. It's okay to be less than perfect. Who cares?! Have fun. Allow yourself to play, enjoy, and let loose.

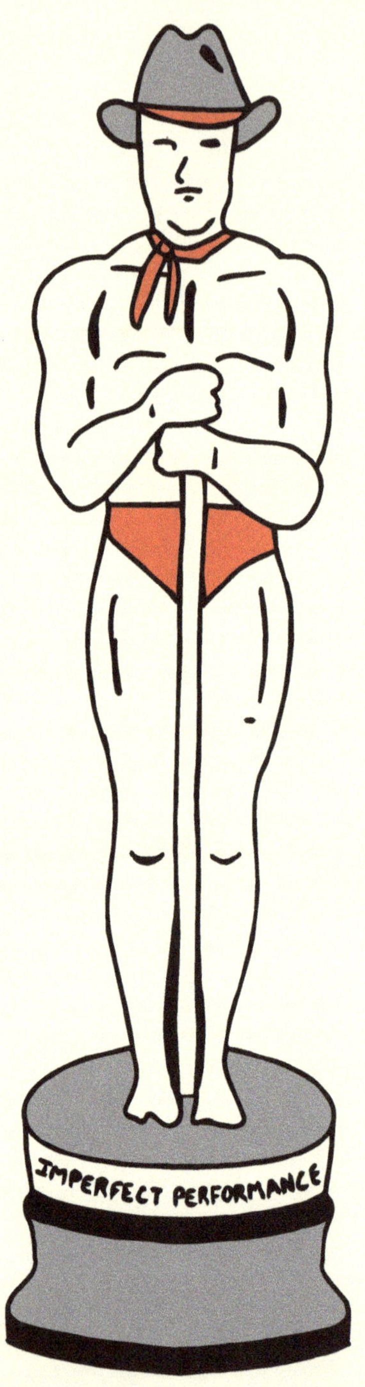

20

Instead of worrying about how you will be perceived, place your attention on something other than yourself: focus on your audience, your insights, your wisdom, and your unique perspective.

Strength Training

Public Speaking is a skill that everybody has the muscle to develop.

Rule of Three

Three Bears, Three Musketeers, Three Stooges . . . the rule of three is a powerful tool based on the principle that our brains recognize patterns. Three is the smallest number of elements required to create a sequence. In comedy, for instance, two isn't enough to make us laugh and four is too many. Magic happens in threes.

Research shows that people—including the speaker—can remember only three points. Your audience's comprehension and ability to retain your message are based on their cognitive load. Recognizing the power of the rule of three underscores the importance of keeping your main points to three throughout your presentation. This will reduce your mental burden and avoid overwhelming your audience with excessive information.

I.
II.
III.

Should AI Write Your Speech?

The night before Martin Luther King delivered his historic "I Have a Dream" speech, he gathered with seven close advisors in his hotel room to put the final touches on it. The following morning, copies of his "finished" speech were delivered to the press. King was slated to speak last on that historic August day. After eight hours in the sweltering D.C. heat, Dr. King approached the podium and addressed his heat-exhausted audience.

Somewhere in the seventh paragraph, Dr. King had a brief pause. In that silence, Mahalia Jackson, MLK's favorite gospel singer standing just to the left and behind King, shouted, "Tell 'em about the dream, Martin!" In that fleeting pause in time, history was changed forever.

Dr. King set aside his prepared script and, in the spirit of the moment, began: "I have a dream that one day this nation will rise up and live out the true meaning of its creed: 'We hold these truths to be self-evident, that all men are created equal.'"

Now, imagine if AI had generated his speech.

"I project a future where this nation will elevate and actualize the core principle of its vision. Furthermore, that everyone should experience equitable treatment through innovative and transformative solutions."

In an era where a computer can write our speeches for us, it is very tempting to use AI. Just plug in a few keywords, and *shazam*—your work is done. Yet, if you listen closely, how many times have you sat through a graduation speech, a corporate presentation, or even a wedding toast where you turn to the person next to you and say, "This is insulting to listen to this AI-generated nonsense. If I have to listen to the words 'effective,' 'furthermore,' or 'innovation' one more time, I'm gonna pull my hair out."

That's because speaking isn't just about words; **it's an exchange of energy** between you and your audience—a dialogue. This exchange is a conversation that carries a vibration. Audiences can sense the difference. Before you give AI a chance to write your speech, PLEASE STOP: There is no substitution for what comes from your heart. Your voice is irreplaceable. We want to hear what YOU have to say.

Lincoln vs. AI

Lincoln's Words:	AI's Interpretation:
"Four score and seven years ago our fathers brought forth on this continent, a new nation, conceived in Liberty, and dedicated to the proposition that all men are created equal."	"Eighty-seven years ago, our ancestors embarked on an innovative journey to establish a new nation on this continent, effectively founded on the principles of liberty and equality for all."

Avoid the Slide

The philosopher Wittgenstein once said, "If you can't say it, point." I say, "If you can't say it, then and *only* then, show a slide!" We've all experienced it: the presenter reading every word on the slide; the font being too small to see, or having to sit through a YouTube video. (Zzzzzz . . .) As attention drifts, people begin turning off their cameras.

> People who know what they're talking about don't use PowerPoint.
>
> —Walter Isaacson, author of biographies "Steve Jobs" and "Leonardo da Vinci"

Research shows that PowerPoint presentations can literally shut down our brains. Studies have demonstrated that excessive use of text-heavy slides leads to cognitive overload, making it difficult for the audience to process and retain information.

My suggestion: Only use a slide if what you're trying to communicate cannot be conveyed through words alone, such as when you require a bridge from one idea to the next.

The real power lies in your words. Instead of relying on slides, try a metaphor or storytelling approach to make your point.

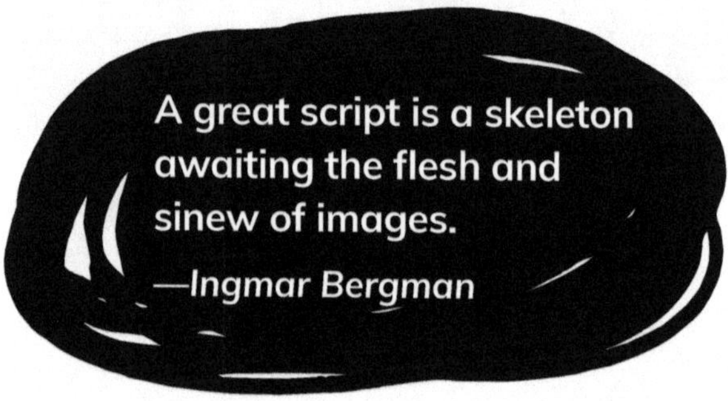

A great script is a skeleton awaiting the flesh and sinew of images.
—Ingmar Bergman

Part One

(Crafting what to say in under 5 minutes)

T**his part of the book** introduces the SPEAKEASY Method™: A quick and fun approach to speech writing that makes everything much less scary (and much more fun)! All you need is a piece of paper, a pen and an open mind.

Note: From this point forward, I will typically refer to your speech as your script.

After nearly a decade of teaching public speaking at Colorado Mountain College using the traditional approach, one evening, I said to my class, "Okay, now it's time to learn how to write a speech," and handed out the standard outline. The energy drained from the room as if I had betrayed them. In a simple twist of fate, I instructed my students to take a piece of paper, fold it into thirds, and create a tic-tac-toe board. The rules were: there are no right or wrong answers, work quickly, work with an open heart, and no second-guessing yourself.

Method to the Madness

Let's begin by looking at the elements that make the SPEAKEASY Method™ work so well.

RAPID PROTOTYPING

A prototype is the simplest possible execution of a design concept. Here, it will be the simplest possible version of your script. As game designer Will Wright describes a prototype; it is "a navigation instrument . . . It's a compass."

Rapid prototyping for presentations is like sketching a rough outline and then building it quickly without worrying yet about perfection. Using the SPEAKEASY Method™ alleviates the pressure of coming up with all the key points independently and forces our creativity to be *automagically* activated.

Your aim will be to work as quickly as possible to build something that can be experienced and learned from and then move on to other design aspects. During the prototyping phase, remain open to discovering moments of fun and engagement within the experience, regardless of their initial triviality or seeming nonsensicalness.

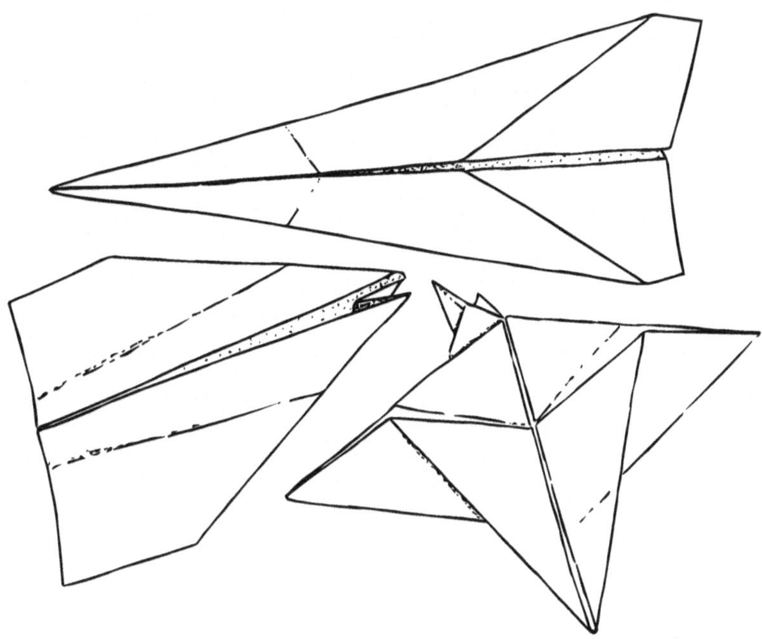

EXQUISITE PRESSURE

When you're ready to begin creating your prototype, you will work under a five-minute time constraint.

We've all experienced working under deadlines and witnessed seemingly miraculous results. Trusting your initial response becomes more natural under pressure because your mind doesn't have time to think, analyze or judge. Research suggests that performing under pressure allows brain regions associated with creativity to become more active, bolstering imaginative thinking and problem-solving abilities.

Magic unfolds with limited thinking and minimal discussion. Exquisite pressure serves as a catalyst for creativity. Without a predetermined outcome in mind, you're poised to uncover extraordinary, serendipitous moments of discovery that might otherwise be missed without the constraint of time.

NON-SEQUENTIAL THINKING

Non-sequential thinking, or non-linear thinking, refers to the cognitive process where ideas, information, or events are not connected in a linear or chronological order. It involves the ability to process, understand, and link information in a way that does not strictly follow a step-by-step progression.

When working in a non-linear way, which you will with the SPEAKEASY Method™, you can make connections between unrelated concepts, ideas, or experiences. This allows for a more creative and abstract approach to problem-solving because you can see relationships and patterns beyond a straightforward sequence.

This type of thinking enables us to consider multiple perspectives or solutions that might not otherwise be immediately obvious.

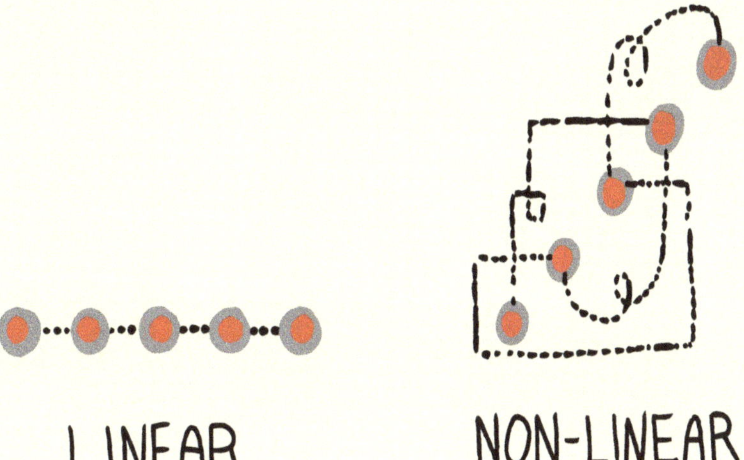

FREEWRITING

Freewriting, or stream-of-consciousness writing as it is sometimes called, is writing about the first thing that comes to mind for a set amount of time without interruptions or self-editing. Your task is to let the words flow without analysis or judgment. Working this way may feel unnatural at first; don't stop, keep going. While freewriting, you will train your brain to work more spontaneously.

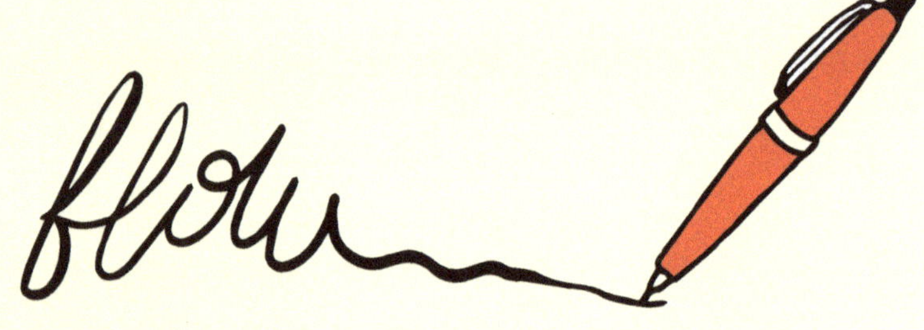

LANDSCAPE MODE

Portrait mode on your phone is perfect for scrolling social media feeds and reading. However, it has its limitations. It restricts the amount of information you can see at any given time. It doesn't give you the complete picture. We stream movies, watch videos, and play games in landscape mode because it gives us a broader view, making it more interactive and less linear. Landscape mode allows you to see more of what's in front of you.

We're going to rotate our paper from the normal portrait orientation to landscape mode when doing the SPEAKEASY Method™ because turning the paper sideways allows you to open yourself to a new perspective, shakes up the way we usually do things, and makes it more fun and game-like.

Creating Your Prototype

You're going to build the prototype for your speech on a grid of nine boxes/sections. I'll give you a prompt for what goes in each section of this grid. When the grid is complete, it will be the map of your speech and will be read in a linear or sequential manner (top-to-bottom and left-to-right). However, the order I'm going to instruct you to fill in the sections with answers to my prompts will **not** be sequential. This is how you'll see the magic of non-linear thinking at work!

Exquisite pressure will be applied when you give yourself just five minutes to complete the prompts. Your written answers will be done in the manner of freewriting. Remember to use your prototype paper in a landscape orientation to create for yourself the best view.

# ✳ A Note on 5 Minutes

The SPEAKEASY Method™ is designed to work in 5 minutes. The first few times may take a little longer because you're reading the directions, but don't let that added time make you overthink things. It's normal to feel confused at first. Don't let reading the directions slow you down. This isn't about being perfect; it's about the genius that comes from speed. Let go of all the predetermined ideas you have. Spontaneity and happy accidents happen under this exquisite pressure. You'll be surprised by the ideas and insights that emerge.

R U Ready?

NINE SQUARES

Take a standard piece of copy paper (or any paper large enough to write on) and with the paper oriented horizontally (landscape mode), take your pen and draw a grid that divides the paper into thirds each direction—three columns and three rows. Or, you can fold the paper into thirds each direction to have fold lines as a reference.

TEAR OUT THIS PAGE

Use the reverse side of this page as a reference for the prompts. The prompts are also included on the pages to follow, but this at-a-glance sheet will support your creative flow, making it easier to work through the steps.

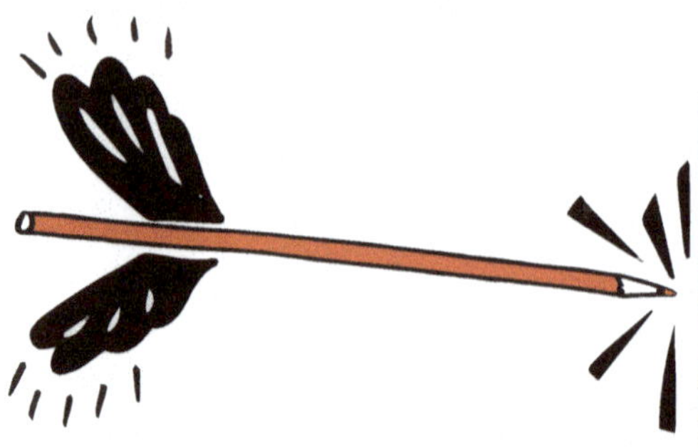

SPEAKEASY
Prototype Cheat Sheet

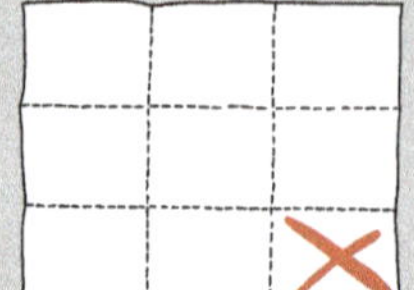

Prompt 1:

THE ONE THOUGHT - Write "*If I can leave you with one thought*" and beneath that, jot down the primary thing your audience should take away from your speech. Conclude with "Thank you."

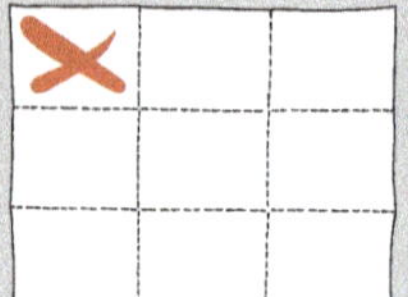

Prompt 2:

COMPELLING SNIPPET - Write an attention-grabbing snippet such as a thought-provoking story, personal anecdote, or inspiring quote. Write out only a few key words to make it easy to remember.

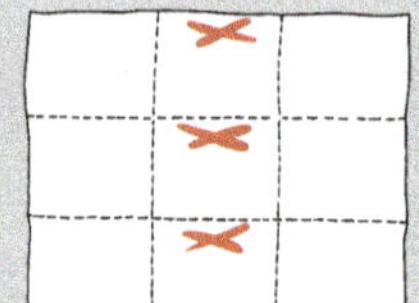

Prompt 3:

THREE HEADLINES - Create one headline for each of the three boxes in the middle row. These are your top three presentation topics. Think of these as enticing teasers to pique your audience's curiosity.

Prompt 4:

HEADLINES' INTRO + SUMMARY - At the top right hand box, write "*To recap, we talked about:*" and list your headlines. In the lower left-hand box write: "*Today I want to talk to you about:*" and list once again your headlines.

Prompt 5:

YOUR PROFILE + ISSUE - In the left-hand middle box write "*Hi, I'm ____*" and write a brief profile to showcase your credibility. Add "*This has led me to the burning question:* [as relates to your topic]" or "*Here's the problem:*" [your problem] *and here's what I see as the solution:*" [your solution]"

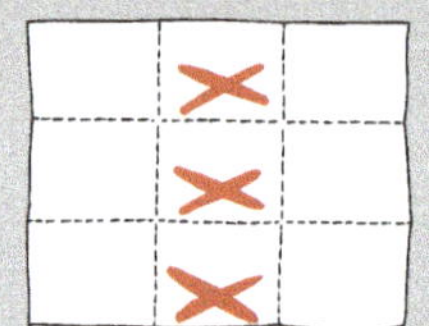

Prompt 6:

HEADLINE STORIES - Return to the middle boxes and add a few sentences under the headlines to create compelling teaching points that explain your headlines.

Prompt 7:

CALL TO ACTION - In the right-hand middle box, write and complete: "*My hope is that when you leave here, you will:* [action you want from your audience]." This can be as simple as "*Subscribe,*" or more specific, such as a prompt to take a detailed action to engage further with you.

The Rules

- Work fast
- Be spontaneous
- Spelling/grammar do not matter
- Stay open-minded (no right or wrong answers)
- Let go of any self-judgment
- Embrace the exploration of new ideas
- Have fun

Grab a timer—your phone works—set it for 5 minutes and complete prompts 1-7.

Prompt 1: In the bottom right-hand box, write "*If I can leave you with one thought*" and beneath that, quickly jot down the primary thing you hope your audience would take away from your speech. In terms of length, think of this as a Tweet or, even better, as a fortune cookie.

Conclude with "*Thank you*" at the bottom to express your appreciation for your audience's attention.

This is a short and powerful message that encapsulates what you want your audience to remember.

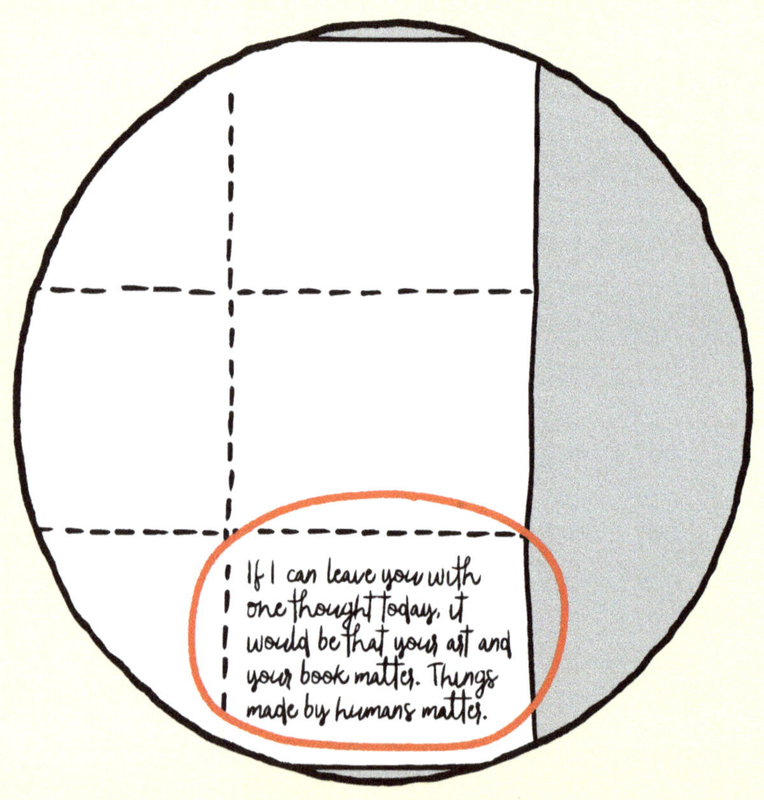

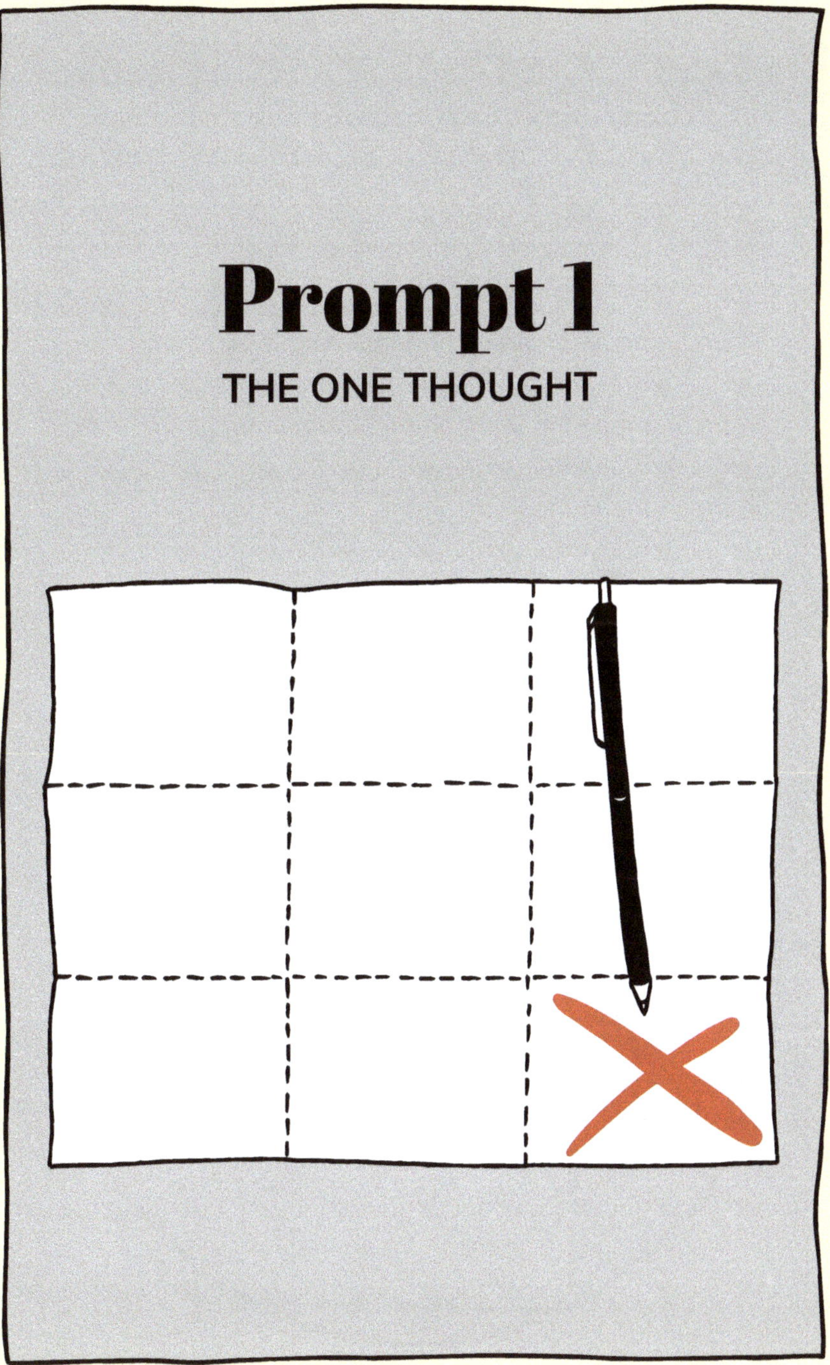

Prompt 1
THE ONE THOUGHT

Prompt 2: In the top left-hand corner box, write an attention-grabbing snippet. Imagine this as an Instagram story—
captivating and something that leaves a lasting impression.

This could be a thought-provoking story, a personal
anecdote, an inspiring quote, or even lyrics from a meaningful song that resonates emotionally with your audience.

Don't spend time writing out the entire story now;
a few key words to make it easy to remember are fine.
You'll have the chance to refine/expand on this in the next
section of the book.

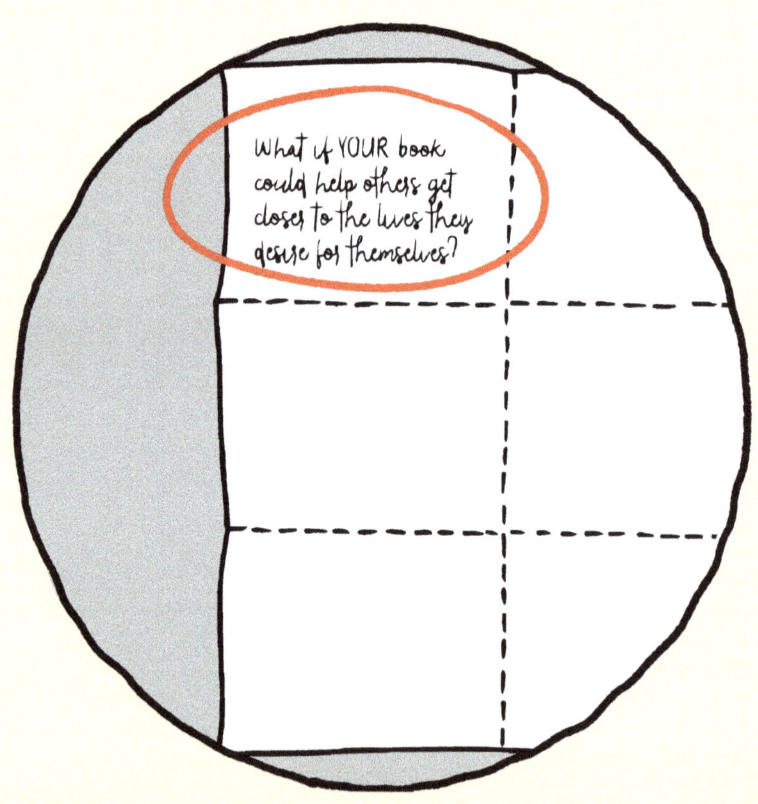

Prompt 2
COMPELLING SNIPPET

Prompt 3: Next, create one compelling headline for each of the three boxes in the middle row. These are your top three important presentation topics.

Think of these headlines as enticing teasers such as clickbait on a YouTube video or a newspaper headline. The goal is to pique your audience's curiosity and entice them to pay close attention to the valuable and interesting content you are delivering.

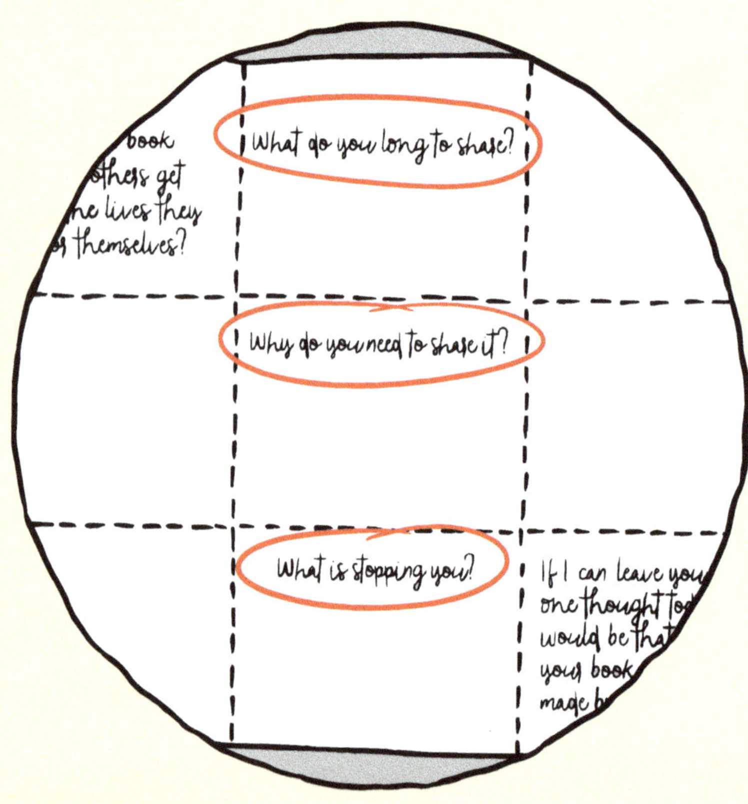

Prompt 3
THREE HEADLINES
THREE BOXES

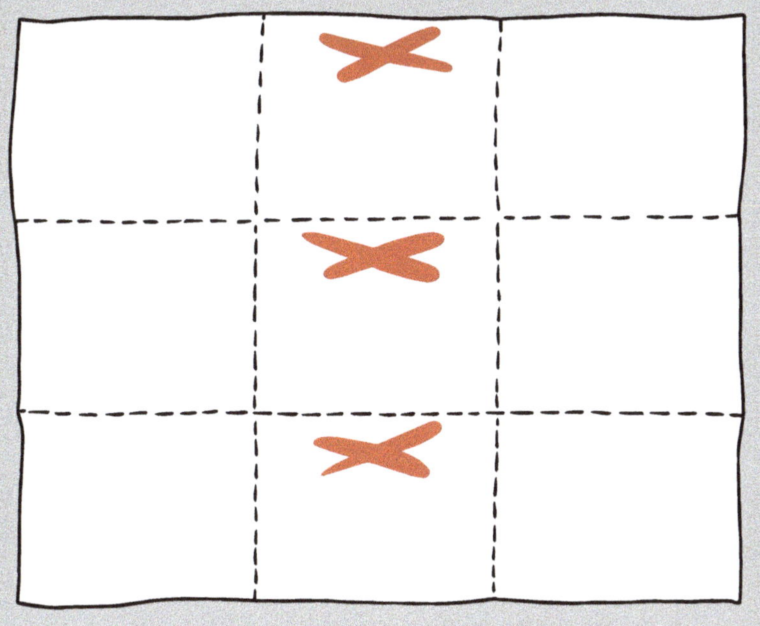

Prompt 4: At the top of the top-right hand box, write
"***To recap, today we talked about:***" and then below that, list
your three headlines from the previous step.

In the lower left-hand box and write: "***Today I want to talk
to you about:***" and below that, list once again your three
headlines.

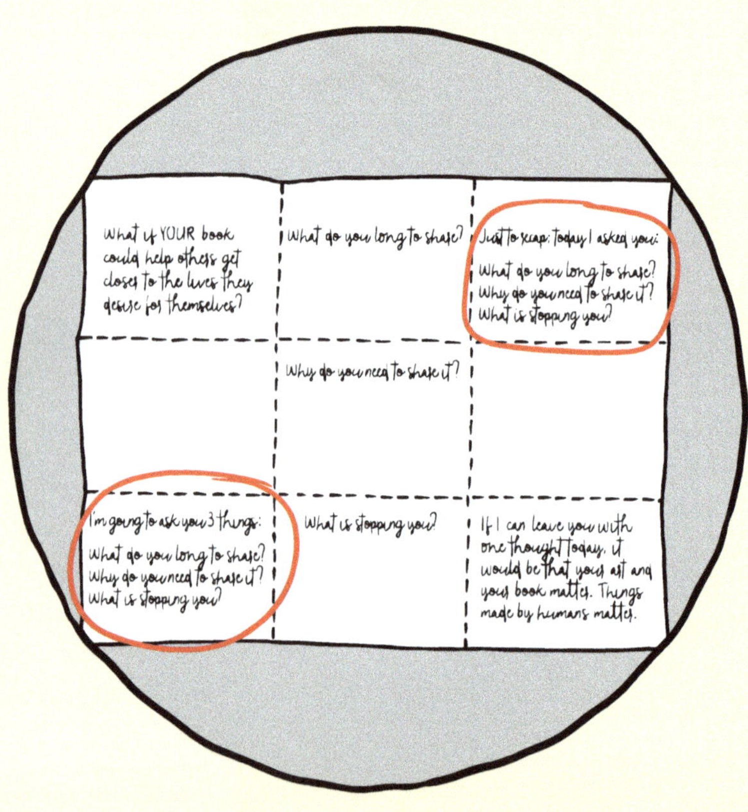

Prompt 4

THREE HEADLINES
TWO MORE BOXES

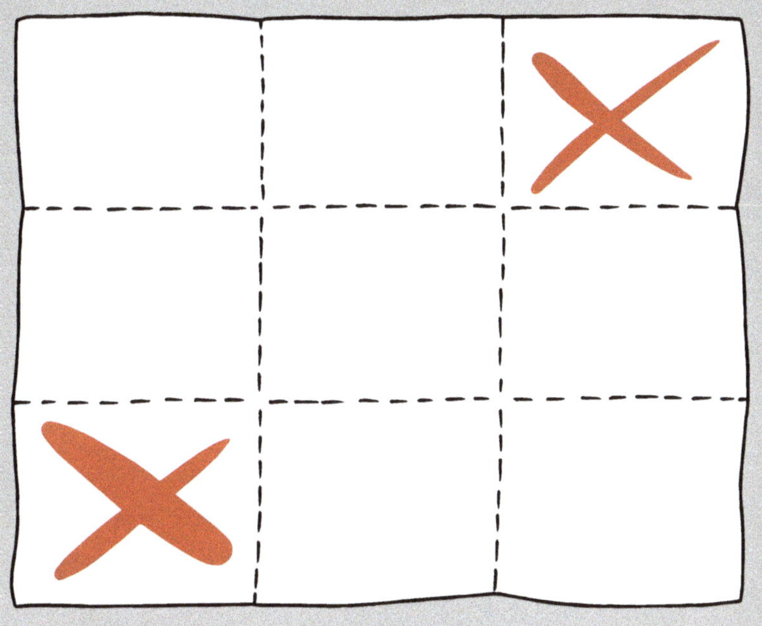

Prompt 5: In the left-hand middle box write "***Hi, I'm [YOUR NAME]***" and then write a brief profile—similar to what you might have on LinkedIn—that showcases your credibility.

Add "***This has led me to the burning question: [QUESTION THAT RELATES TO YOUR TOPIC]***" or "***Here's the problem: [PROBLEM YOU WISH TO ADDRESS] and here's what I see as the solution: [YOUR SOLUTION]***."

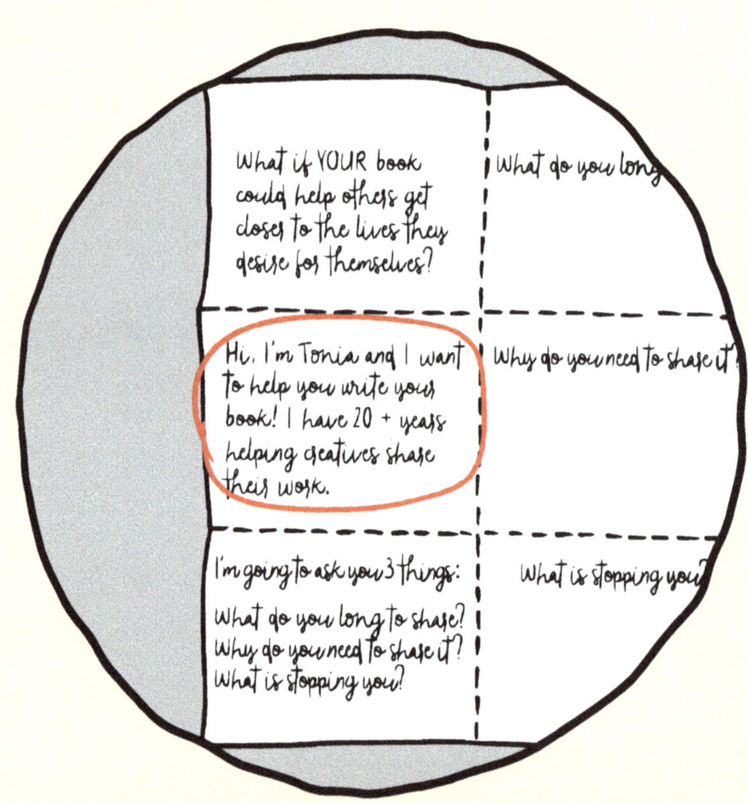

Prompt 5

YOUR PROFILE
YOUR ISSUE

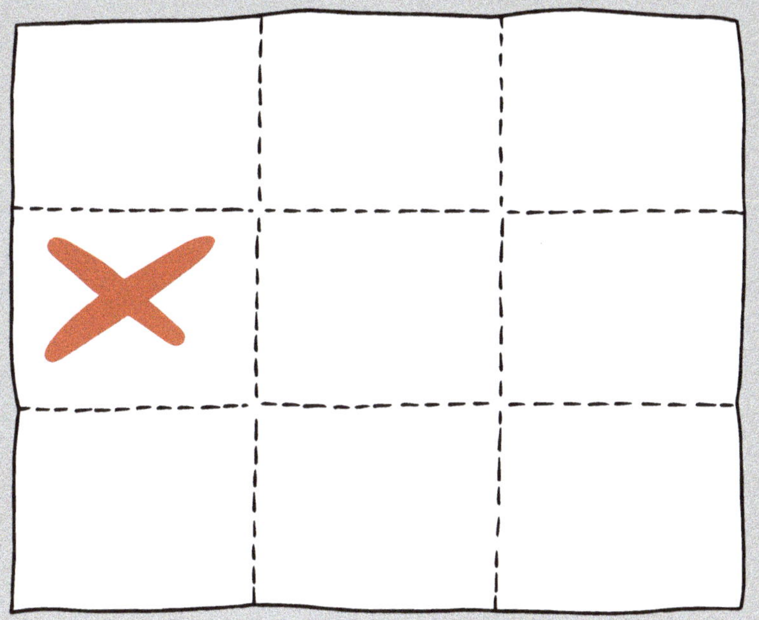

Prompt 6: Imagine you are creating a captivating YouTube or TikTok video. You already have the three headlines that will label the three parts of this topic. Return to the top middle box and add a few sentences under the headline to provide highlights of that section. Repeat for the center and lower boxes of the middle row, adding a few sentences to sum up the highlights under each headline.

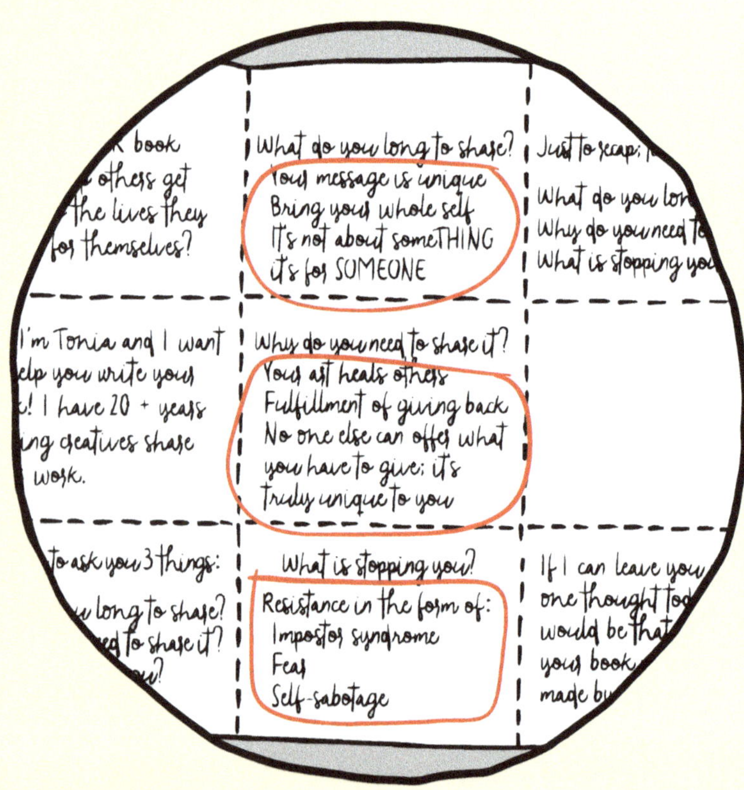

Prompt 6
STORIES UNDER
THE HEADLINES

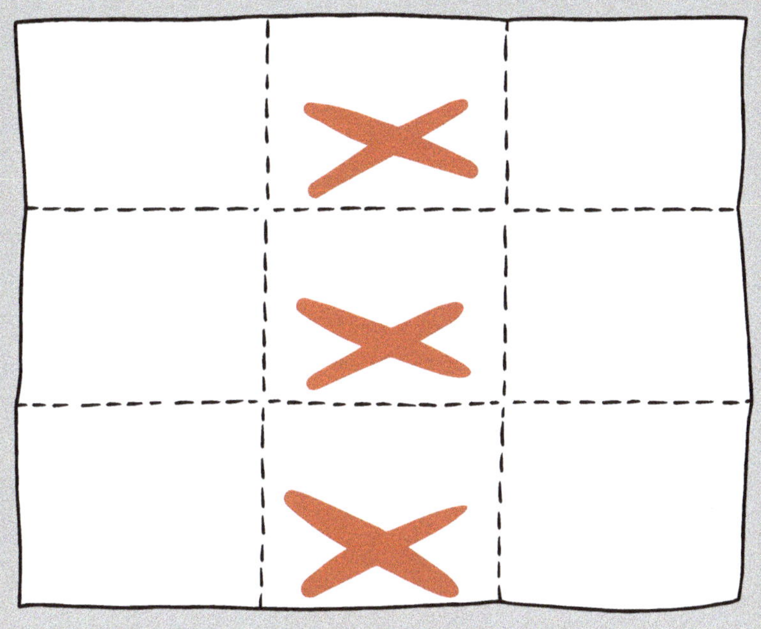

Prompt 7: In the right-hand middle box, write and complete this sentence: "*My hope is that when you leave here, you will [ACTION YOU WANT FROM YOUR AUDIENCE].*"

This is your CTA or call to action—how you let your audience know what they can do after the presentation. It can be as simple as a single word, such as "Subscribe," or it can be a more specific action, such as a prompt to take a detailed action and engage further with your message.

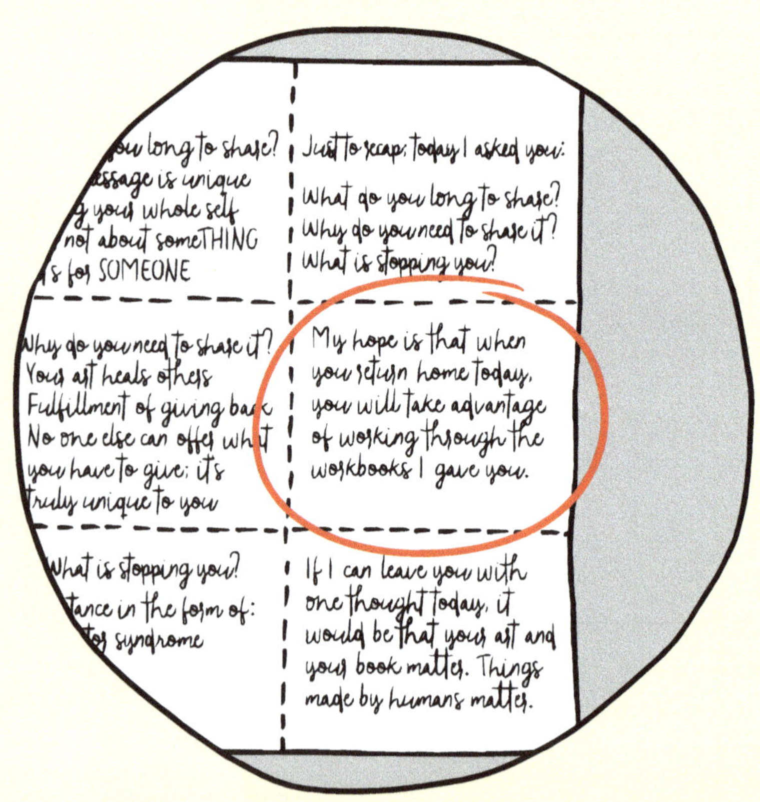

Prompt 7
CALL TO ACTION

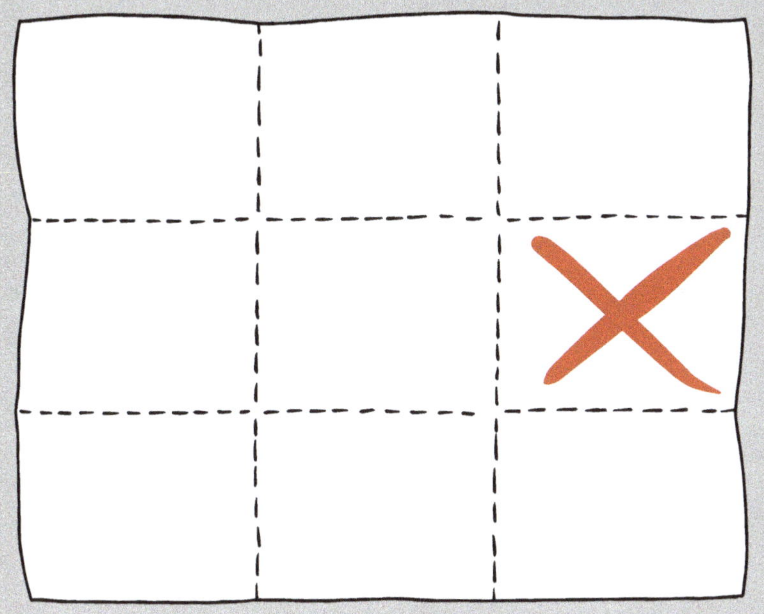

Congratulations!

You've written your speech! What's next?

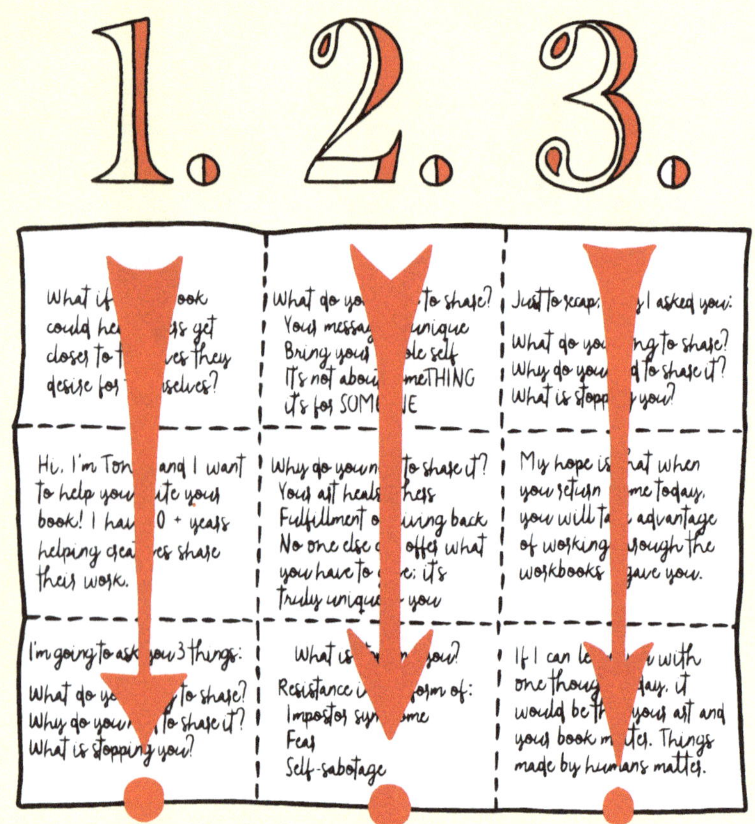

Read down the columns, left to right.

It's Time to (Read) Your Speech!

1. Grab your phone—right now; don't wait.

2. Record yourself delivering the speech.

3. Trust what you've written.

4. Begin by reading down each column of your speech, starting at the top left column, reading down, then reading down the middle column, and finally, reading down the last column.

5. Stick to what you have written.

6. Resist the urge to add commentary. If you didn't write it, don't say it.

7. Remember your speech starts with a hook, NOT: "Hi, my name is_____; today I'm going to talk about . . ."

8. Skip prefacing each segment (box) with an introduction like "Let me start with a quote" or "I'm going to share a story."

9. Riff only on the content you've already written down.

10. Avoid introducing anything new toward the end of your speech. Doing so can confuse your audience and dilute the impact of your core message.

11. End with "Thank you!"

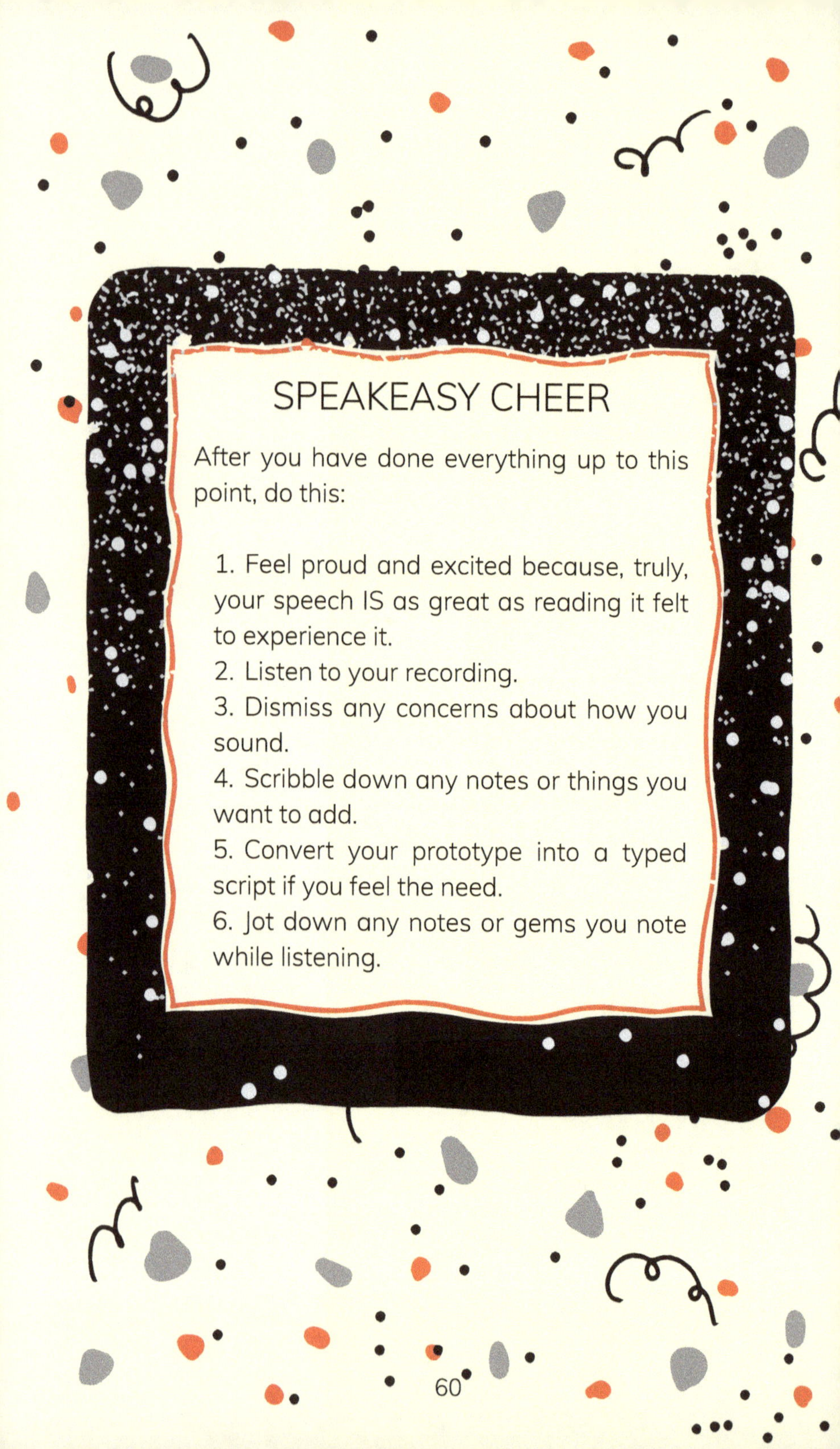

SPEAKEASY CHEER

After you have done everything up to this point, do this:

1. Feel proud and excited because, truly, your speech IS as great as reading it felt to experience it.
2. Listen to your recording.
3. Dismiss any concerns about how you sound.
4. Scribble down any notes or things you want to add.
5. Convert your prototype into a typed script if you feel the need.
6. Jot down any notes or gems you note while listening.

The job is the same – to attempt to make it sound like you've never said it before and as if it's just occurred to you. And that's the same whether you're on camera or whether you're on stage in a room full of people.

— *Bill Nighy*

Part Two

Action Plan

(Methods to ensure you'll be memorable)

In **Part One**, I shared with you how to turn the traditional outline structure upside down in the prototype phase. Now, it's time to flip it back and organize it, as well as devise an action plan so that you feel confident about what you will do when you go to deliver your speech.

Part Two is all about refining and optimizing your script, ensuring it is clear, concise, and unforgettable.

The strategies you will learn in this section will naturally boost your confidence, reduce anxiety and help you stay focused during your presentation. You're going to get hands-on with your script. You'll draw arrows, make slashes, and add symbols and signs to make it more visually engaging and easier for you to follow.

As you're refining and fleshing things out, remember the Rule of Three and stop at three main attractions—your three headlines—to avoid overwhelm. Instead, you will keep them wanting more; to run up to you at the end of your presentation, hungry for what's next. But, at the same time, you don't want them to feel starved because you didn't feed them enough or because you fed them generic AI rubbish.

Your Mission

The first step for your speech is to get very intentional about the message—your mission—for your presentation. You will do this by simply identifying the *circumstances* of your presentation and who your *audience* is.

The circumstances are the where, why and how. They include the location, reason for speaking, who invited you and whether it is a live or virtual format.

And next, the who. Who is your audience? Consider the audience's size, taking into account whether it's a small gathering or a large crowd. Evaluate the level of formality expected in your speech, considering whether it's a casual setting or a formal event. Assess how open and welcoming the audience is likely to receive your message.

For instance, you are asked to give a toast at your best friend's wedding.

Circumstances: You're toasting your best friend's love at their outdoor wedding. So you'll be using a microphone. **Audience**: Wedding guests (a happy group filled with love and libations).

Grab a notebook and pen or pencil, and do not over-think this. This is a quick scribble; the first thing that comes to mind. Trust your first instinct; you can always go back and update your response. For now, go with your initial impulse.

Complete the following statement for your speech:

My circumstances are:________________________

My audience is:________________________

WHAT DO I WANT?

Once you've established the audience and circumstances of your speech, the next step is to determine your mission and objective. What is the purpose of your speech? What is your intention in your message? And how does it contribute to the overall conversation or the current narrative—the context in which you're delivering your speech?

MISSION

Your mission is your ultimate goal—the driving, motivating force behind your actions. Your mission is your overarching vision, loftiest ideal or your quest.

OBJECTIVE

Your objective, however, is a specific goal you seek from your audience. It's the short-term win, the prize, something you want right away and without delay.

Here's an example. Let's go back to your best friend's wedding toast. You know the circumstances and audience:

You're toasting your best friend's love at their outdoor wedding in front of a happy group of friends and loved ones who are filled with love and libations.

Mission: To honor their relationship and enduring love.
Objective: To congratulate the newlyweds, express your well wishes and heartfelt sentiments.

Your WORDS
+
you
=
Something
GREATER:
your
MISSION

Here are other scenarios:

SCENARIO #1: ADDRESSING CITY COUNCIL

Circumstances: You live in a peaceful mountain town. Investors want to build an airport nearby, threatening your town's charm.
Audience: Members of the City Council (may be hostile).
Mission: To preserve the unique charm of your small town amidst rapid development.
Objective: To convince the City Council to reject the airport proposal and seek alternatives for sustainable growth.

SCENARIO #2: KEYNOTE SPEECH AT A CONFERENCE

Circumstances: You are an environmentalist speaking at a conference about the harmful effects of fracking on the environment.
Audience: Conference attendees, including industry professionals and environmentalists (preaching to the choir).
Mission: Save the planet.
Objective: Persuading policymakers/industry leaders to support renewable energy policies and take action to stop fracking.

SCENARIO #3: EULOGY

Circumstances: You're at a relative's funeral service, paying tribute to a loved one who has passed away.
Audience: Mourners and family members (heartbroken and forlorn).
Mission: To honor their life and legacy.
Objective: To share memories and provide comfort to grieving family and friends.

Now, complete the following statement for your speech:

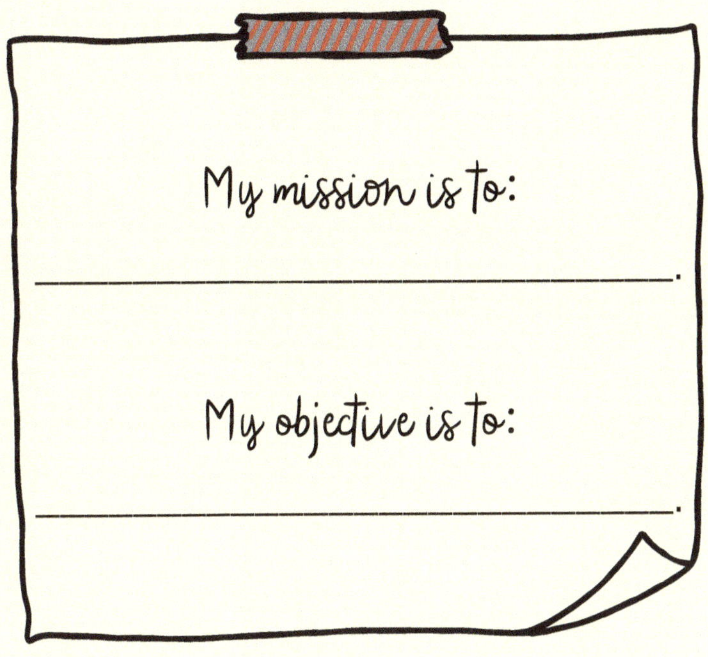

Keep your mission and objective at the top of the page onto which you'll write your speech. (Or write it on a sticky note that you can put at the top or move around.) If you ever feel off track, scared, or lost during your presentation, you can quickly remind yourself of your intention. It's like a mini-cheerleader.

Script Scoring

What is script scoring?

Script Scoring is a system of notating your script, based on how you plan to deliver it during a live performance.

Music often springs to mind when talking about script scoring. Composers write music with specific notes telling musicians how to play it. For example, the notes are played short and separated into pieces marked with a **staccato** symbol (•). Similarly, a **crescendo** symbol (>) indicates gradually increasing volume, while *piano* (p) signifies playing softly. And when you see *fortissimo* (ff), it means to play very loudly.

This is exactly what you will do for your script. You will use your own set of scoring symbols to indicate how certain words or phrase should be spoken. For instance, to mark a change of thought, you'll use: (/) for a beat, (#) for a pause, (☺"emoji") to denote emotion and (+) for action.

These symbols will serve as guideposts, helping you navigate your performance with clarity and precision, ensuring your message hits the right notes with your audience. If you're the type who enjoys color coding, feel free to use different colored markers for the various scoring practices.

Sectioning

I want to guide you through the process of breaking your script down into logical sections as well as bite-sized pieces to allow you to treat each section of your script with the care it deserves.

The first thing to do is to organize your script into three acts and nine scenes, like a mini-movie or TV show. The three columns of your prototype serve as three acts—the beginning, the middle and the end—and the individual boxes will represent scenes. Each scene will build on the next to tell a story that supports your mission. If you're using the original working draft prototype, take a pen and label the top of each section with Act I, Act II, and Act III.

ACT I	ACT II	ACT III
What if YOUR book could help others get closer to the lives they desire for themselves?	What do you long to share? Your message is unique. Bring your whole self. It's not about someTHING it's for SOMEONE	Just to recap; today I asked you: What do you long to share? Why do you need to share it? What is stopping you?
Hi, I'm Tonia and I want to help you write your book! I have 20 + years helping creatives share their work.	Why do you need to share it? Your art heals others. Fulfillment of giving back. No one else can offer what you have to give; it's truly unique to you	My hope is that when you return home today, you will take advantage of working through the workbooks I gave you.
I'm going to ask you 3 things: What do you long to share? Why do you need to share it? What is stopping you?	What is stopping you? Resistance in the form of: Impostor syndrome Fear Self-sabotage	If I can leave you with one thought today, it would be that your art and your book matter. Things made by humans matter.

If you have a printed copy of your script, simply draw a horizontal line to separate each section of text and write the following where the breaks are (in the margin if necessary): Act I, Act II and Act III.

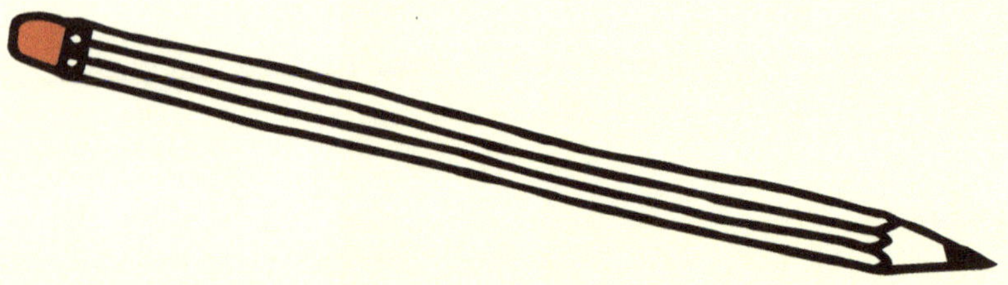

Beats

A "beat" is an opportunity to take a pause in your presentation. Beats manage the pacing, tone and crucial points in your speech in order to allow what you're saying to sink (or sync) in with your audience.

A new beat signifies a change, such as a shift in topic, tone or thought. This includes moments such as delivering a key point, introducing a new idea or transitioning between sections.

MARKING BEATS

Grab a pen. Use a forward slash (/) to mark beats. This helps highlight changes in purpose, emotions or shifts in your storyline. You should end up with nine or more beats—one for separating the "scenes" of each box you filled in for the prototype, plus any additional ones you may feel are needed.

What if YOUR book could help others get closer to the things they truly desire?
• 2003 - incredible gift of Divine grace, I had landed a job with a publisher for art/craft books.
• I didn't have an English degree . . .
• A maker my entire life, craft-book fanatic for years, yet still suffered IMPSOSTOR SYNDROME //

Hi, I'm Tonia Jenny and for 20 years now, I've been supporting visual artists, crafters and makers in getting their messages of inspiration out into the world—primarily through the outlet of book publishing. //

I want to present you with three questions:
- What do you long to share with others?
- Why do you need to share it?
- What is stopping you? //

What is it that you long to share with others?
• Mark Twain—there are no original ideas; Michael Crichton — "Books aren't written, they're rewritten."
• Granular level, your art has an inherent message - uniquely yours.
The best topic for your book – a sweet spot that comes from a combination of your values + passions; your learned knowledge + skills and your natural gifts.
• Your book isn't about something; it's for someone. Your work has its own message. //

Why do you need to share your message?
• May I take a stab at answering this for you? On a deeper level, you want to share it because whatever the message is, it has been a source of your own healing.
• You long to give back; to leave something of yourself behind to live on after you.
•No one else can share your topic in your way—your perspective, your experience. //

What is stopping you?
FEAR
•Impostor syndrome! (Author- or artist-impostor syndrome.)
•Self-sabotage
•Overcoming resistance – You're an artist, not a writer. Your idea has already been done. You're not really all that great at your craft . .
Your belief about not being capable or credible could run a little deeper into your subconscious and could express in more insidious ways through excuses: //

To summarize then, we've looked at three things to consider when it comes to the book within you:
- What is the message of inspiration behind your work?
- The importance of your unique brand of expression.
- How to address your limiting beliefs resulting from impostor syndrome. //

My hope is that when you return home today, you will take advantage of my free gift to you and download the two workbooks for The Book Within You. That you'll be excited to get started on your publishing journey. Give the seed of inspiration a chance to sprout and bloom. //

If I can have shifted your perspective on one thing today, I would hope it's that your art—and the beauty it contributes to this world—matters. Art and beauty matter. Things made by humans matter. A book featuring your work is something that can live on and continue to uplift and support others long after you are gone. Thank you for listening and letting me share these insights with you. //

Most young people haven't used their storytelling skills since they were 8 or 9 or 10 and wanted to persuade Mom and Dad to take them to the ball game.

— Peter Guber, NY Times bestselling author of *Tell It to Win*

Actioning

Have you ever watched a scene in a movie where the actors are so crafty, they can woo, persuade, manipulate or cajole another character into doing something? They're secret is "actioning," and that's what you're about to learn.

Now that you've identified your objectives, you'll spice things up by using actioning techniques—a panacea for public speaking that helps you overcome monotony and achieve your objective.

THE BIKE ANALOGY

Imagine a child who desperately wants a bike. Their immediate goal or objective is clear: They want their parents to buy them a bike. But beyond just getting the bike, their mission is bigger—they really want freedom and a sense of independence.

Now, the question is, how are they going to persuade their parents to buy them a bike? The child will try various tactics, such as to beg, to demand, or even to charm their parents into buying them a bicycle. How might the child employ actioning to get what they want? Depending on the tactic (verb)—beg, demand, charm—the child's voice, facial expression and body language would be different.

 PRACTICE ACTIONING 

First, just say, "Mom, can you buy me a bike?"

Now try saying the above sentence employing the following verbs:

- As if you are trying **to beg** someone to get you a bike.
- As if you want **to demand** they get you a bike.
- As if you want **to charm** them into getting you a bike.

Notice how your voice automatically changes, as does your calmness/demeanor. For a brief moment, I bet you were able to get out of your head and put your attention elsewhere.

This is your aim: To focus on your objective (not how nervous you might feel) and achieve it.

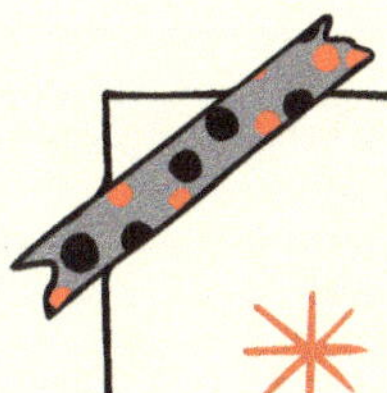
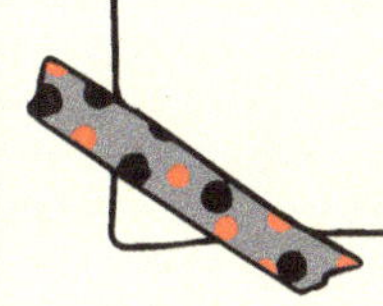
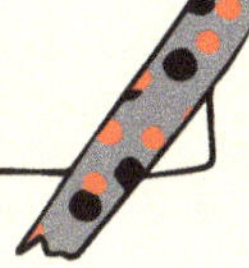

HOW TO SCORE YOUR SCRIPT FOR ACTIONING

Using a contrasting color pen/marker, make a plus sign (+) followed by your desired verb in all caps at the beginning of the phrase/sentence you want to apply actioning.*

See the Appendix for a list of actioning verbs.

+ TO EXCITE
Introducing our innovative product, the "EcoTech Energy Saver!" + TO HOOK This groundbreaking device is designed to save you money while revolutionizing energy consumption in households. + TO LURE With its smart sensor technology, the EcoTech Energy Saver monitors and optimizes energy usage, reducing waste and ultimately cutting utility bills. + TO TEMPT Its sleek design and user-friendly interface make it a must-have for environmentally conscious consumers seeking efficient, cost-effective solutions. + TO ENCOURAGE Experience the future of energy conservation with the EcoTech Energy Saver!

Emotion

Once you've applied actioning, it's time to add emotional depth. Emotions are at the heart of every decision and action that drives us. This is true whether you are trying to persuade someone to join your cause or convince them to change their thinking. Emotions often override logic. Emojis can be used as a tool to mark up your speech to indicate how you want your audience to feel throughout different beats.

Conveying emotion, especially in presentations, has historically been taught as a no-no. We've been told to be objective and detached. An exception might include joy in a wedding toast or sorrow in a eulogy. But for the most part, we've been taught to suppress emotion, leaving us playing one note, making for dull and unanimated talks. We're now going to change that! Permission granted to express a range of emotions.

EMOJIS

Humans have expressed themselves pictorially for eons to convey emotions. From ancient hieroglyphics to the tiny symbols we send on our phones, these images allow us to communicate complex emotions with a single icon. Most of us agree that emojis are an emotional thesaurus, helping us express feelings that words alone cannot capture.

Every time we send an emoji, we express empathy. For example, when a friend shares happy news, we send a smiley face; when we receive sad news, we send a heartbreak emoji. Whether it's something funny, exciting or magical, emojis allow us to transfer heartfelt expression of our emotions to others.

Let's tap into that and add another layer of ways to

connect with your audience using empathy and emotions.

"A picture's worth a thousand words." Cliché but true!

SCORING YOUR SCRIPT USING EMOJIS

Start by reading your script without any preconceived performance ideas, as if someone else had written it. Then, jot down your immediate feelings about the following questions:

- What emotions do you want your audience to feel?
- How does the script resonate with you on a personal level?
- What emotions does your script evoke? For instance: excitement, curiosity, worry, fear, motivation or any other specific emotions.

Now, as you did with actioning, draw emojis to each beat or paragraph to add another punch to your script.

For example, when discussing happy news, add a smiley face emoji to convey your excitement. Similarly, when discussing a difficult situation, add a sad face emoji to express empathy and understanding.

What if YOUR book could help others get closer to the things they truly desire?
• 2003 - incredible gift of Divine grace, I had landed a job with a publisher for art/craft books.
• I didn't have an English degree . . .
• A maker my entire life, craft-book fanatic for years, yet still suffered IMPSOSTOR SYNDROME //

Hi, I'm Tonia Jenny and for 20 years now, I've been supporting visual artists, crafters and makers in getting their messages of inspiration out into the world—primarily through the outlet of book publishing. //

I want to present you with three questions:
• What do you long to share with others?
• Why do you need to share it?
• What is stopping you? //

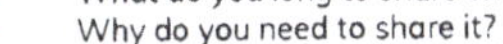

What is it that you long to share with others?
• Mark Twain—there are no original ideas; Michael Crichton — "Books aren't written, they're rewritten."
• Granular level, your art has an inherent message – uniquely yours.
The best topic for your book – a sweet spot that comes from a combination of your values + passions; your learned knowledge + skills and your natural gifts.
• Your book isn't about something; it's for someone. Your work has its own message. //

Why do you need to share your message?
• May I take a stab at answering this for you? On a deeper level, you want to share it because whatever the message is, it has been a source of your own healing.
• You long to give back; to leave something of yourself behind to live on after you.
•No one else can share your topic in your way—your perspective, your experience. // 

What is stopping you?
FEAR
•Impostor syndrome! (Author- or artist-impostor syndrome.)
•Self-sabotage
•Overcoming resistance—You're an artist, not a writer. Your idea has already been done. You're not really all that great at your craft . .
Your belief about not being capable or credible could run a little deeper into your subconscious and could express in more insidious ways through excuses: //

To summarize then, we've looked at three things to consider when it comes to the book within you:
• What is the message of inspiration behind your work?
• The importance of your unique brand of expression.
• How to address your limiting beliefs resulting from impostor syndrome. //

My hope is that when you return home today, you will take advantage of my free gift to you and download the two workbooks for The Book Within You. That you'll be excited to get started on your publishing journey. Give the seed of inspiration a chance to sprout and bloom. //

If I can have shifted your perspective on one thing today, I would hope it's that your art—and the beauty it contributes to this world—matters. Art and beauty matter. Things made by humans matter. A book featuring your work is something that can live on and continue to uplift and support others long after you are gone. Thank you for listening and letting me share these insights with you. //

Other Scores

Choreographing every element of your speech, like pauses, questions, and when to take a sip of water, can really help you manage the flow of your presentation. For instance, you can use a water glass icon [🥛] as a cue to take a sip and pause after an important message. This might seem trivial, but it gives your audience time to absorb what you've said and gives you a moment to gather your thoughts before starting your next point. Have you ever watched a comedian take a sip of water after a joke? It gives them a beat to let the laughter build and the audience a moment to reset before hearing the next joke.

TEMPO

Sometimes nerves get the best of us. Tempo is all about how fast or slow you speak. On a scale of 1 to 10, how fast do you talk? One is really slow, ten is hyperspeed. Personally, I'm around a 7. My exuberance can get the best of me, so when I'm on the radio, I use Post-It notes that say, "Slow down" and "Give it a beat" to remind myself I'm speaking too quickly.

Here's how to find your natural speaking pace: Start reading your script aloud at a medium pace and call that a 5. Slow it down to a 2, like you're barely moving through quicksand. How does that feel? Then, speed up to a 10, like a football player doing drills. Dial it down to a 7 and feel the difference.

This exercise helps you gauge your vocal tempo. Mark your speech with a number for the pace you want. If you're speaking too fast, slow down; if too slow, speed up.

QUESTION/PAUSE

Anytime you ask a question—rhetorical or direct—mark your script with a big [?] Then, use that as a reminder to yourself to pause for three seconds while your audience contemplates what you've asked. This pause might feel like an eternity, but it's important for your listeners to have this time. This pause sets the pace and helps the audience travel along with you. It also helps you gauge their response.

VOLUME

As presenters, we often stick to a comfortable grey zone where everything sounds the same. Once upon a time, we had to project our voices to reach the back of the auditorium. Now, the new "back of the room" is often across the computer screen. Think of your speech as a wave, which rises and falls in intensity.

Mark your script with an arrow [∧ or ∨] to indicate the volume level you want. While some parts are louder, make other parts softer to make your audience lean in and listen.

Practice with a mic if you plan to use one. (See more in *Part 3, Tech Rehearsal*).

EMPHASIS

Because you want variety, mark your script by underlining the important words you want to emphasize. Draw a bold line under words you want to stress.

Only perfect practice makes perfect.

—Vince Lombardi

Rehearsal

(Bringing your speech to life)

Raise your hand if you rehearse in front of a mirror. Do you record yourself and then nit-pick your appearance or how awful you think you sound? Do you ask your family to volunteer as your audience? If you do any of these, you're not alone. What you may not realize about rehearsing this way is that it can be counterproductive.

In Part Three, I will teach you how to rehearse effectively to ensure that you are prepared and ready to step in front of an audience with confidence and purpose.

Practice makes permanent. We'll build your confidence by mixing repetition with creativity and fun, letting you loosen up and enjoy yourself. Make "Practice as you play and play as you practice" your mantra. So, let's forget the old way and just have a blast with it!

What IS Rehearsal?

Rehearsal is a time for exploration and discovery. It is not just about memorizing lines; it's about the intentions of your presentation. It's a process of experimentation, refining, and shaping the performance to convey the desired message and intended impact to the audience.

It is important to create a safe and supportive environment during rehearsals, where you feel free to take risks, make mistakes, and explore different possibilities.

Now that I've helped you established the importance of practice through rehearsal, it's time to **bring your speech to life** by walking through the scenario as realistically as possible. Instead of merely going through the motions, you'll actively move around, speak out loud, visualize the space and recreate the atmosphere where your audience will be. Practicing this way will help reduce nerves and uncertainty.

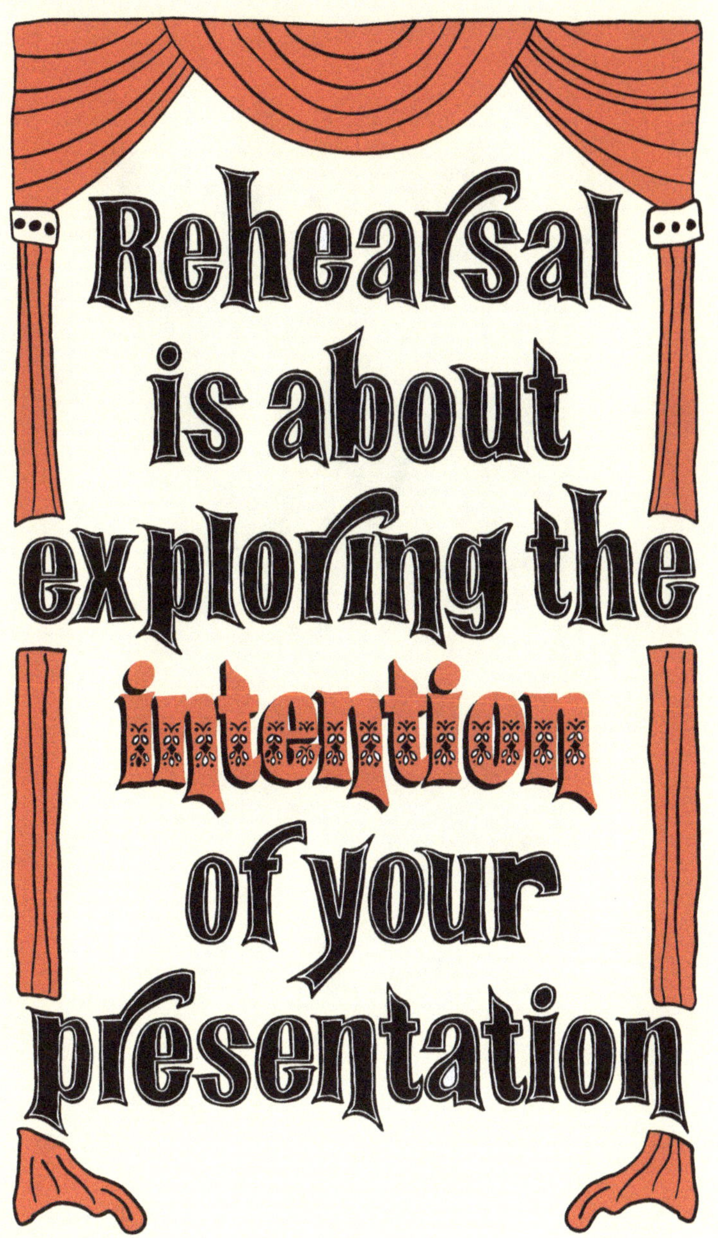

Rehearsal
is about
exploring the
intention
of your
presentation

Rehearsal 1

SETTING THE STAGE + BLOCKING

Recreate Your Space

If you can't physically rehearse in your future performance space, do your best to recreate it as accurately as possible, in a quiet and comfortable space—preferably not in front of the mirror—where you will not be disturbed. Ideally, it should be a room where you have space to play and let loose.

Begin by visualizing the platform—will you present via a Zoom call, in a classroom, a theater or at a podium? Rearrange chairs to represent your audience or place your computer where you will be performing. Anything you can use to simulate the space is beneficial.

Put on your director's hat for this. Step back for a moment and envision your production. In your mind's eye, picture where your presentation position will be. Consider any technological requirements, such as audio and lighting. The more you can visualize the space and brainstorm everything you need for your presentation environment, the smoother your rehearsals will run and, in turn, your performance.

Gather and Arrange Props

Next, arrange props—things such as your computer, charts, handouts and a water bottle. Determine your distance from the audience (virtual or physical) and plan your positioning.

You can use pretend objects such as a hairbrush, a pen, or even a toy microphone to mimic holding a mic while rehearsing your speech or performance. Get creative and imaginative: Move around chairs to simulate a mock audience and place stuffed animals or action figures in the chairs as your listeners.

Once this is completed, move on to blocking, which involves determining positions and movements.

Troubleshoot Everything in Advance

Use this list to help you determine things you may never have even considered. Answer the following questions.

1. Where will you perform? _______________________
2. Where will you enter? _______________________
3. Is your performance on Zoom? (Yes/No). If yes, where will you be seated?_______________________
4. Do you need a podium? (Yes/No)_______________
5. Will there be any restrictions on movement or space during your performance? (Yes/No)
6. Will you require a microphone? (Yes/No)

BLOCKING TIPS

Blocking refers to where to stand or where to move during a performance. Planning specifics on where to move can be an effective way to help express the plot and subtext of your message. Examples:
- Standing at the podium
- Where you are entering and exiting from
- Stepping in front of the podium for emphasis

Blocking

Once you have set up your stage, the next step is to plan out every single step of your presentation. Start by imagining where you will be entering the stage or room for your pitch or board presentation. Now, walk to that spot and feel what it feels like to stand there in the moment before you enter. Will there be someone to introduce you? If so, picture being backstage or in the wings while you wait for your entrance.

Maybe you are speaking at a city council meeting and will be called up from the audience. Imagine walking up to the podium to address the audience. Or will you be on a dais, clinking a glass to propose a wedding toast?

Take note of all your movements and write them down in your script, including your exits. Here are some abbreviations you can use to mark your script:

- EN - enter
- X - cross
- EX - exit
- H - pass out handouts
- CL - click new slide

For example, EN - walk up from the audience; stand and clink glass; EN SL (enter from stage left) - walk to podium; X - stage to click slides; X H - cross stage to pass handouts.

Physically walk through your script multiple times until you feel comfortable. Practice these movements until you feel at ease; annotate all your movements in the margins of your script using a pencil. Writing this down reinforces the movement, ingraining it into your physical memory. Over time, these movements become second nature, much like learning a sport or dancing.

Of course, it isn't essential that you move around. You might be at a lectern in front of a packed auditorium with all the lights and sound provided, or you might be in your bedroom on a virtual call. If you are in your bedroom, make sure that your desk and lighting are preset properly. (A budget-friendly ring light can be your best friend.)

Here are a few tips: don't get backlit (light behind you that creates a silhouette). Instead, turn your desk to face the window for natural light. And think twice about using that phony beach background that makes you look like you're floating in space when you step out of the frame. It's unnecessarily distracting.

Connection WITH YOUR CAMERA

When presenting virtually, audiences often miss the subtleties of nonverbal communication. One way to address this is by leveraging your camera as a tool. Filmmakers use techniques like close-ups to zero in on emotional cues.

The "shot," as it's called, refers to where the camera is located. The placement of your camera can reveal the level of closeness or distance between you and your audience. The farther the camera is from you, the speaker, the more distant the audience will feel. Mark your script, depend-ing on the effect you want to achieve; choose the shot that works best for your presentation. Consider physically leaning in at certain moments to establish closeness or to reveal emotion and vulnerability.

A medium shot is popular on television as it captures gestures and body language but may not clearly con-vey emotions. This may be what you use as your default distance from your camera.

Close-ups, in which you lean into the camera to show only your face, can show intimacy and make a closer connection between you and your audience, allowing them to better un-derstand your emotions or highlight an important point.

Rehearsal 2

THE MUMBLE-THROUGH

Getting Familiar with Your Script

Hopefully, you're feeling more comfortable already. Being on your feet and in your body is the best way to get out of your mind and feel less anxious about being in front of people.

Now, you are ready to pick up the script and rehearse it. If you can, give yourself about one hour for this rehearsal as well as Rehearsal 3—The Stumble-Through. I suggest not going through your entire speech from beginning to end in the initial practice; it can be exhausting and not necessarily helpful at the start. Keep your nose buried in your script if necessary in the beginning rehearsals. Slowly but surely, you will rely on your script less and less.

After several run-throughs, you will notice that somehow, you will automatically start to remember your lines, and with that, you will also develop an air of confidence.

Keep in mind that during rehearsal, you are not going for performance but for familiarity, understanding and building muscle memory. Rehearsing is all about learning and refining your performance. Take your time, rewind, and practice as much as you need. Each repetition helps you become more confident and polished. Don't hesitate to go back, fix any mistakes, and keep practicing until you feel comfortable and prepared. You've got this!

Review Your Script

Review your script again before you jump into rehearsal to ensure it's organized into acts and scenes. If it's not already structured this way, take some time to organize it now. (See *Part Two*.) Next, re-familiarize yourself with your choices: Identify your objectives, actions and the emotions you want to convey to the audience in each scene. Make sure you have marked them in your script. Confirm that the room is set up to simulate your presentation environment. Double-check that you have all your props, technical requirements, and, most importantly, a glass of water.

The Moment Before or 'Pre-Beat'

Your speech starts before you even step on stage, so it's important to give yourself a moment to pause and gather your thoughts before starting. The "pre-beat" refers to the moment just before you, the performer, go on stage or begin a performance. It's a preparatory moment during which you can mentally and physically prepare to enter the arena.

Think of the skier at the gate, a pilot before takeoff, the actor standing in the wings. During this time, the performer may focus on getting into character, adjusting their mindset and ensuring they are emotionally and mentally prepared to engage with the audience.

The pre-beat is an essential technique for cultivating the appropriate energy and presence prior to entering the spotlight. It serves as a bridge, enabling a seamless transition from the realm of everyday life to the heightened reality of the stage.

The Mumble-Through

Here it is—the big moment you've been preparing for. It might feel daunting, but once you start speaking, you'll find it gets easier. This is what's called the "mumble-through."

A "mumble-through" rehearsal is a stress-free practice session in which you familiarize yourself with the script and experiment with your delivery without the pressure of perfection.

During a mumble-through, you can speak your lines softly or even mumble them to yourself as you work your way through your speech, hence the name. This rehearsal is all about exploring your material, finding your voice, and understanding the flow of your talk without worrying about memorization or precise delivery. It's an opportunity for you to get comfortable with the speech and begin shaping your performance before diving into more intensive rehearsals.

So, if you are ready, grab your script and pencil, and let's get started.

As I mentioned earlier in the chapter, I suggest avoiding going through your entire script in one go. Instead, break down your rehearsal into smaller, more manageable chunks. Start by practicing Act 1, scenes 1–3, then take a break before moving on to Act 2, scenes 3–6, followed by another break. Finally, rehearse Act 3, scenes 7–9.

Go over each part individually twice before attempting to run through the entire script.

Mini Rehearsal Schedule

1. Review script structure: 5 minutes
   - Ensure the script is broken down into acts and scenes. If not, organize it now.
   - Go over your blocking.
   - Identify objectives, actions, and desired audience emotions for each scene.

2. Practice acts—each act individually twice: 45 minutes
   - Act 1, scenes 1-3: 15 minutes
   - Act 2, scenes 3-6: 15 minutes
   - Act 3, scenes 7-9: 15 minutes

3. Take breaks: 5 minutes ea

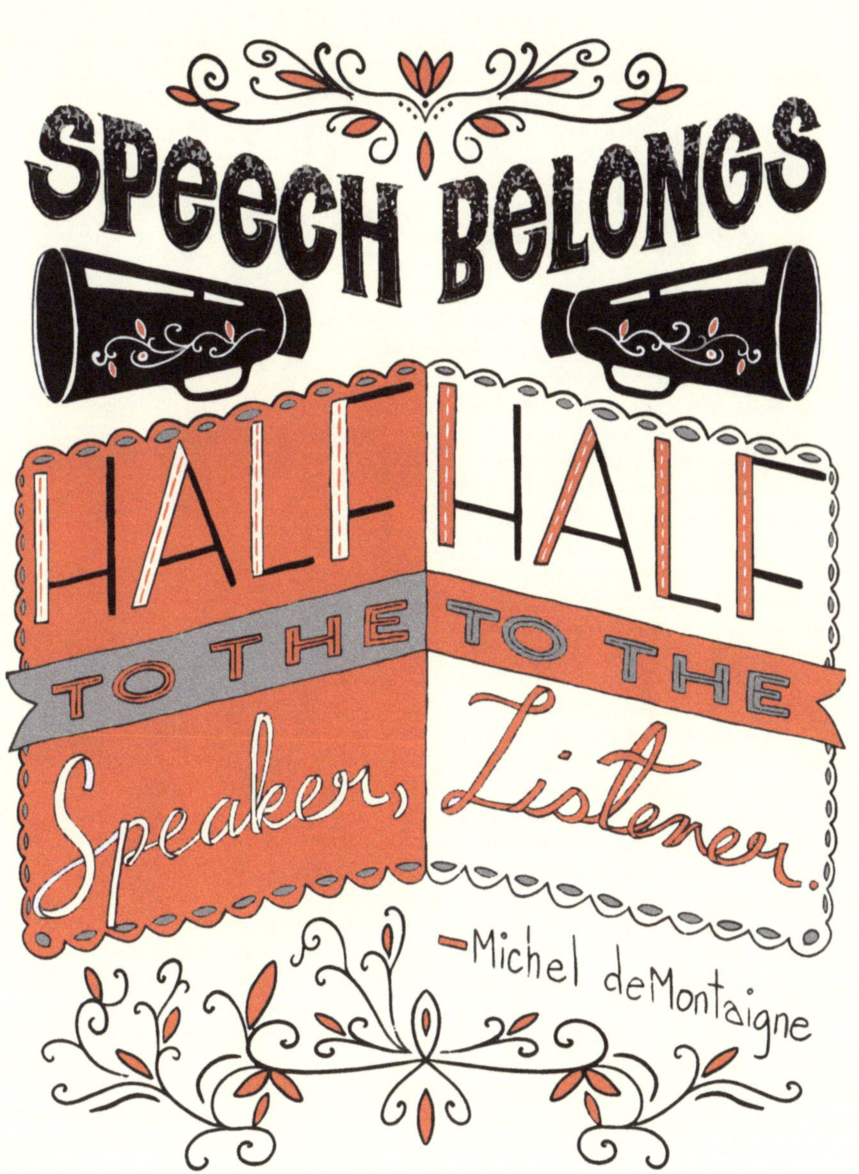

SPEECH BELONGS
HALF TO THE Speaker,
HALF TO THE Listener.
—Michel deMontaigne

Rehearsal 3

THE STUMBLE-THROUGH

Moving right along, you are ready for the stumble-through, an attempt at a full run-through.

It's called a "stumble-through" because the emphasis is on working out all the logistics of movement and position-ing, nailing down your choices, deciding what to leave in, what to take out, and how you will play your actions and emojis. The stumble-through rehearsal helps you learn the flow and pace of your speech and fix any potential issues.

Like the mumble-through, the stumble-through is not about achieving a polished performance. You are still in the exploratory stage, but you are narrowing down and committing to your blocking and other physical movements, such as running through slides and pausing to check in with yourself. You are learning to chew gum and walk at the same time.

The goal of the stumble-through is to go through your entire speech from start to finish. Jot down notes of any stumbling points or areas where adjustments are needed, and then go back and stumble through again.

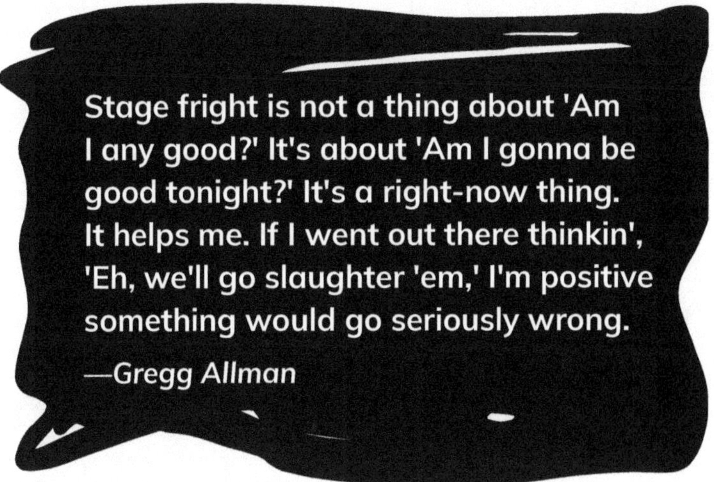

Rehearsal 4

THE RUN-THROUGH

Now, it's time for an official run-through. Hopefully, you are feeling more confident and jazzed about your talk.

A "run-through" is a rehearsal where you go through the entire speech without stopping, aiming for a smoother delivery. It typically occurs after you have thoroughly rehearsed your lines, blocking and cues, and it's used to gauge the flow of your presentation and identify any areas that may need tweaking or adjustment.

Of course, you can still use your script. Always keep it handy. By now, you're probably making significant progress. You might feel more self-assured, depending less on your notes. Challenge yourself to rely less on your script and focus more on speaking directly to your imaginary, stuffed-animal audience.

Expect hiccups, hesitations and rough patches as you navigate your material. But don't stop unless something really goes wrong. You are getting the flow, the timing, the pace and how much energy it requires to get through your talk. Mistakes will still arise, but this is an opportunity for you to reconnect with the original spontaneity of creating the script and applaud yourself for how all the elements are coming together into cohesiveness!

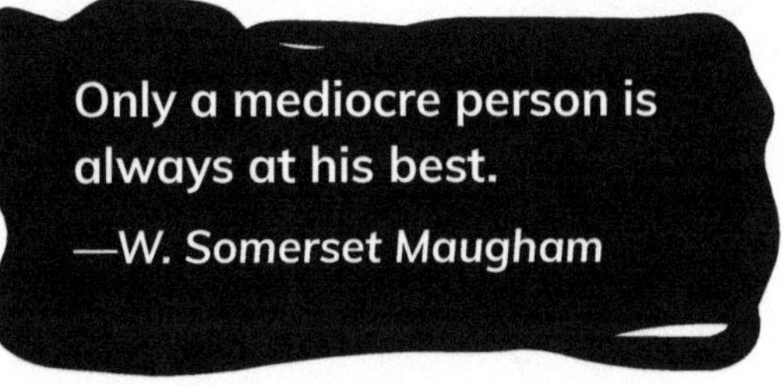

Rehearsal 5

THE TECH REHEARSAL

Congratulations on trying a different way of rehearsing and on committing to incorporating these new techniques into your practice. While everything is going so swimming-ly—and I don't mean to throw a wrench into things—but it's time to consider making sure that everything will go smoothly by getting clear on the technology you'll be using to deliver your performance.

The tech rehearsal is designed to run all the technical parts of your presentation, from having adequate Wi-Fi to making sure your slides are in proper order to knowing your audience can hear you.

Anticipate Murphy's Law—"Anything that can go wrong will go wrong." Be prepared for the projector to stop working, your laptop to die, or your slides to go missing. Technical glitches have become commonplace, yet maintaining composure when they arise is still crucial.

Imagine you are presenting and, at the last moment, you are handed a handheld microphone instead of the clip-on mic you were promised. How will you juggle the microphone, your notes, and your water? Solution: grab a stool and place your notes and water on it.

In the tech rehearsal, start at the top of your script and go through all the technical aspects of your presentation.

If someone other than you will be managing the tech during your performance, meet with them before your talk. Make notes for them and prepare clear communication outlining your requirements.

This checklist is simply suggestive. I recommend making your own, as you're the one who knows what your presentation will require and what you will need to make things easiest and most successful for you.

Don't wait until the day before your event to make a list. You can start a list as early as your first rehearsal and jot down things as they come up.

In best-case scenarios, you can work everything out beforehand. In the worst case, be prepared to roll with it. Remember, it's not the end of the world or a measure of your success. The real test of your success is your ability to adapt, remain calm, and enjoy the experience.

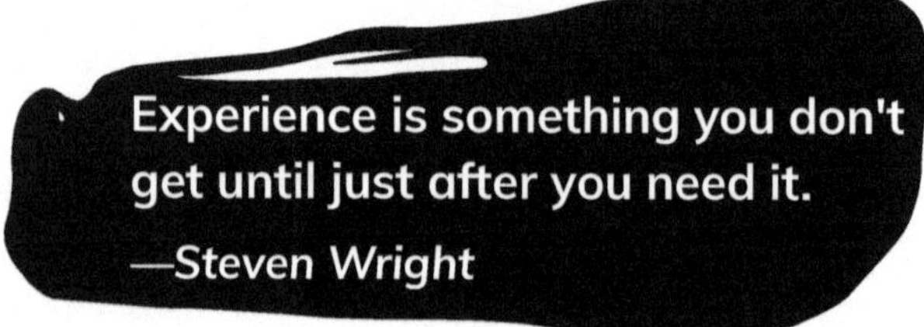

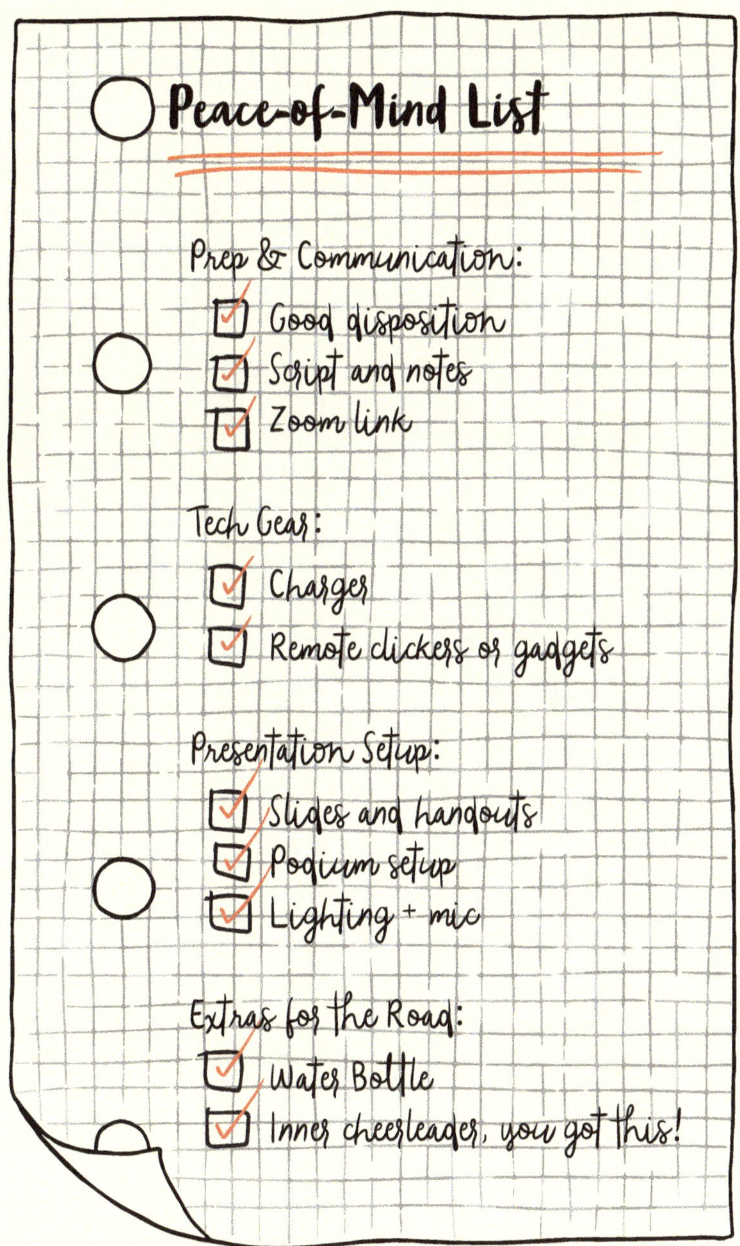

Peace-of-Mind List

Prep & Communication:
☑ Good disposition
☑ Script and notes
☑ Zoom link

Tech Gear:
☑ Charger
☑ Remote clickers or gadgets

Presentation Setup:
☑ Slides and handouts
☑ Podium setup
☑ Lighting + mic

Extras for the Road:
☑ Water Bottle
☑ Inner cheerleader, you got this!

Rehearsal 6

THE DRESS REHEARSAL

A dress rehearsal is a full run-through of a performance, typically done in the attire you will wear for your presentation. It's the last step before the real deal, making sure everything from your attire to the technical aspects blends smoothly with your presentation with no surprises.

Alright, here's the plan: Get ready in what you'll wear for your talk. Treat this rehearsal like it's show day. You'll do a complete run-through of your presentation, from start to finish. No stopping, no shortcuts. You need to feel out your energy. Remember, you practice as you play, so don't expect lightning to strike on the big day, prepare for it instead.

Dress for Success

There's a billion-dollar industry out there that will tell you how to dress for success. We have spent this entire book *redefining* success: Your ability to communicate an idea with your audience. Just as words tailor your message, let your confidence be the stitching that sews it all together for the final performance. Before taking the stage, wear your most comfortable *self*, poised for a sure win!

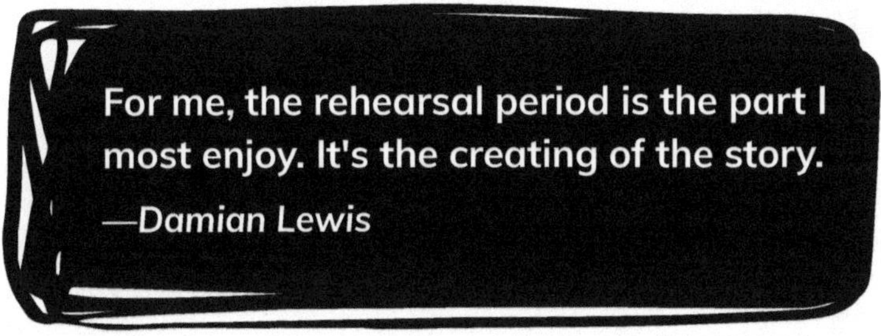

Rehearsal 7

THE PREVIEW

You've worked really hard to reach this point. Inviting someone to watch you can make you feel vulnerable, and it's natural to fall back on old habits and tendencies. Your nerves can get the best of you when you showcase your work in front of an audience for the first time. Will you feel nervous? Yes! Will that out-of-body experience start to happen, and your inner critic start talking louder than you? Yes. Will your face get flushed and feel jittery? Yes. This is normal. So be careful who you ask to be your first audience. Previews are essentially a testing ground to help you adjust your speech based on reactions and feedback from a small invited audience.

Feedback

We all want positive recognition for our work and accomplishments. Go ahead, pat yourself on the back. We also want validation from others for our efforts and what we've done well. So, go ahead and seek that positive feedback, but be intentional in your asking. Here's how you can be strategic in your approach.

Focusing on what constantly needs fixing can breed doubt, insecurity, and uncertainty. While it is important to be aware of problem areas, a mindset steeped in criticism takes its toll and has side effects that blind us to what is good. Training ourselves to look for the positive and praiseworthy takes practice.

You are not seeking approval. You are looking for input on the material you are presenting. Instruct your listener on how to give you feedback by asking whoever is watching you—preferably not a family member or overly critical friend—to take notes. Remember, we are not going for the Oscar; our goal is to plant the seeds of new ideas into the minds of our audience.

INSTRUCT YOUR LISTENER

You can help your volunteer listener(s) *help* you in getting feedback that is truly useful. Hand them a pad you've pre-pared with two columns, hearts and question marks.

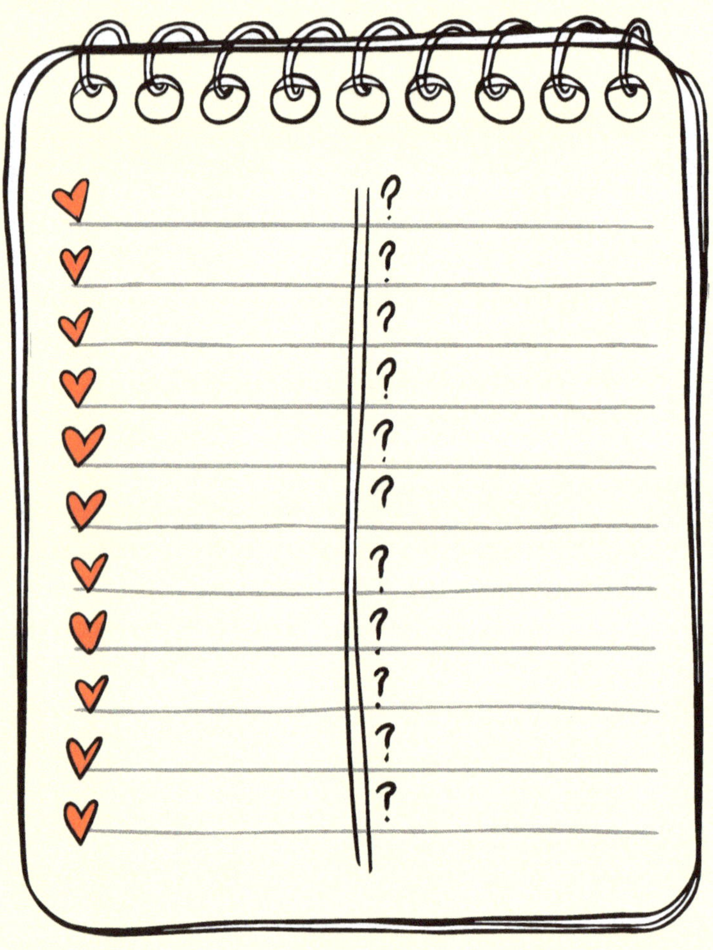

Tell them to write down all the things that they loved next to hearts in the left-hand column and anything they had questions about in the right-hand column next to question marks.

Ask them to be as specific as possible. You can also ask them to watch and listen to areas you are curious about. Direct your listener as to what to pay attention to. The more precise you are in directing their focus, the more attuned they will be to listening to your work.

Here are some examples:

- "When I presented the statistics on climate change, did it make you feel scared?"
- "During the introduction, did my opening story capture your heart?"
- "Were any of my explanations confusing?"
- "Did my visuals help you understand the content better?"
- "Were there parts of the presentation where I lost you?"
- "Did my conclusion leave a lasting impression on you?"

If you ask an explicit question such as, "When I talked about the statistics on climate change, did you feel scared?" Your listener will respond with either yes or no, giving you concrete data on whether your message was impactful. If they respond, "No, I kind of lost you," you know you need to clarify that part of your talk.

Avoid asking your preview audience general questions such as, "How did I do?" This leads to generic answers and potentially harmful feedback. Broad questions like 'How did I do?' or 'What did you think?' open the door to unsolicited advice and unhelpful criticism, such as:

- "It was okay . . . I would have done it differently."
- "I would have added more jokes."
- "You should be louder."

> **You teach people how to treat you by what you allow, what you stop, and what you reinforce.**
> —Tony Gaskins

If you are looking for a performance review, again, be as specific as possible with your questions. Here are a few examples:

- To assess pacing, ask, "Did the pacing of my speech keep you engaged throughout?"
- To gauge tone and pitch, ask, "Did you feel persuaded or have another reaction to my speech?"
- To check your blocking, ask, "Was my walking around distracting to you?"

HANDLING NEGATIVE FEEDBACK.

There's always room for improvement. When receiving feedback, I suggest that you hear the nicest possible interpretation.

Receiving criticism without specifics can feel personal, but don't take it to heart. Take feedback for what it's worth. If your invited audience says, "It was good, but you gotta slow down," instead of thinking negatively, ask them a clarifying question like, "Thank you. Where exactly in the speech did you feel I spoke too fast?"

Ideally, someone might say, "In that section about the waves, you started talking so fast, and I couldn't follow what you were saying."

If you listen carefully, this is specific feedback. What they're really saying is, "It was really interesting, but you were talking so fast, and I wished I could keep up to understand you fully."

Now you have something that you can work to fix. Go back and mark your script to remind yourself to take a sip of water and count to three before continuing.

Then, ask your listener, "Do you mind if I try that section again for you?" Practice that part again, giving specific instructions to your listener to note if they notice a difference the second time.

Show Time!

LIGHTS, CAMERA, ACTION

So, the day has finally arrived. Remember George Spelvin? Well, you are **not** George; you are prepared. You know your lines, you know your blocking and you know your intentions —you're prepared for both the known and unknown.

It's time to set aside everything you've practiced and learned, and trust that all the hard work has paid off. It's time to step into the limelight. Will your hands still shake? Yes. Will your heart still race? Yes. Remember, the adrenaline you feel is proportional to the energy that you need to perform. This nervous energy is the fuel that fills your tank. Nerves and anxiety are no reflection of your preparedness. You got this! I'm over the moon for you.

Drop me a line; tell me how it goes!

TOP TIPS

- Stick to the script you've written.
- Refrain from starting your speech with your "Hi, my name is______." (You'll say it later.)
- Dive straight into your content. Allow what you wrote to speak for itself rather than saying, "Let me start with a quote" or "I'm going to share a story." JUST STICK WITH THE QUOTE or STORY.
- Refrain from the temptation to improvise your speech; it can disrupt and dilute the impact of your message.
- Resist the temptation to introduce *anything* new, especially toward the end of your speech.
- End with Thank you!

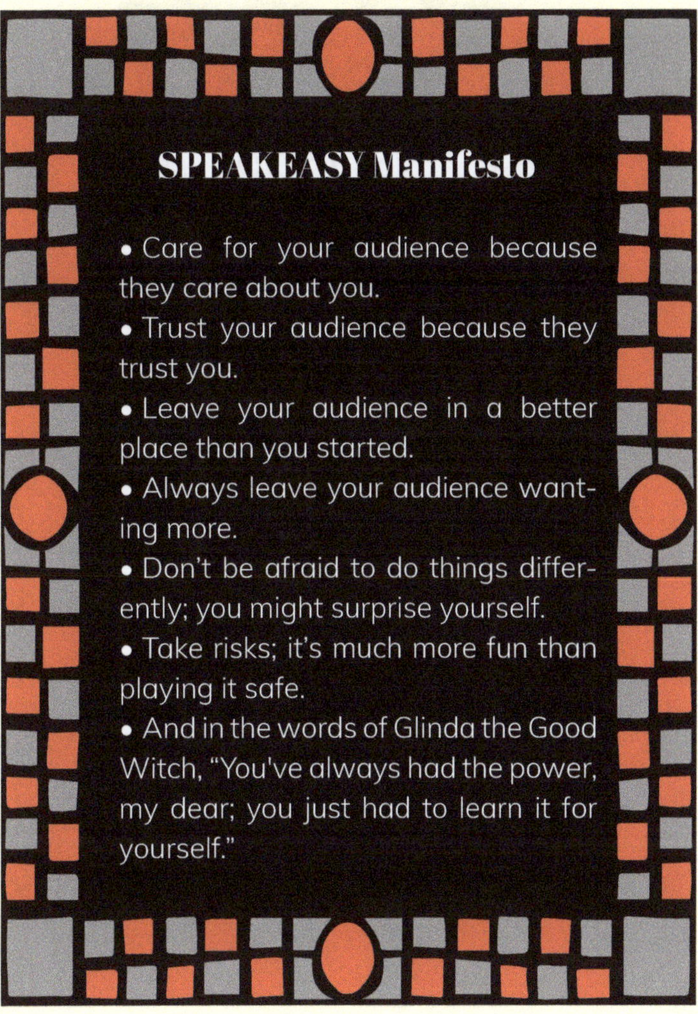

SPEAKEASY Manifesto

• Care for your audience because they care about you.
• Trust your audience because they trust you.
• Leave your audience in a better place than you started.
• Always leave your audience wanting more.
• Don't be afraid to do things differently; you might surprise yourself.
• Take risks; it's much more fun than playing it safe.
• And in the words of Glinda the Good Witch, "You've always had the power, my dear; you just had to learn it for yourself."

YOU did it!

Final Thoughts

Oh, (interjection), I exclaimed when my boss told me I had to give a presentation to the board. I had flashbacks to my first time speaking in public when I was too (emotive adj.) to reach the podium, and the teacher had to pull up a milk crate for me to stand on. I was (emotive adj.). My face turned (color), and all the words (verb ending in ed) from my (body part). I (past-tense verb) I would never speak in public again.

That was until I discovered SPEAKEASY.

Hi, my name is (your name), and today I'd like to share with you the transformative power of (verb ending in ing) my voice and (verb ending in ing) into the spotlight. Let's (verb) into the three key points that have helped me (victorious adj.) my fear.

Firstly, Get the Spotlight Off Yourself. If I learned one thing from SPEAKEASY, it is that the audience is the main attraction. When I stop dwelling on myself and focus the spotlight where it belongs—on my (noun), I automatically, instantly reduce (emotive adj.) stress. Focusing on the audience, you find the true (noun) of connection.

Secondly, Be a Big, Bad Actor. Being a big, bad actor means ditching the (noun) to be perfect. It's about giving yourself the freedom to (verb) up and have fun. Forget about being (adjective). Who cares?! Enjoy the moment, (verb) and let loose. Focus on your (noun), your insights, and your unique (noun) instead of worrying about how you'll be (verb ending in ed).

Lastly, The Power of Being Center Stage. When we speak, our words create (plural noun) that travel through the air, creating (plural noun) that resonate in the minds and hearts of our listeners.

So, there you have it! By focusing on your (noun), embracing your inner (adjective) actor, and harnessing the power of your (plural noun), you can transform your public speaking.

Your voice matters; it's a catalyst for change and a symphony waiting to be (verb ending in ed). The greatest treasures lie within your heart. Unleash, speak, and watch the world resonate with your words.

Acknowledgments

Prior to this book, the SPEAKEASY Method™ was available exclusively to my coaching clients. It worked wonders consistently, but I wasn't sure if that was due to hand holding or if the approach was solid on its own. For years, I tried to draft the process with handwritten directions, scribbles and arrows, but would this method work without me as my clients' personal cheerleader? I didn't know—until Tonia Jenny. I gave the manuscript to Tonia, my editor, who later called and said, "I did the steps, I gave a presentation and it worked!" That's when I knew it was a go.

First and foremost, my deepest thanks and appreciation go to Tonia Jenny—editor, illustrator, collaborator—for making this adventure so much fun. Thank you for your remarkable talent in distilling and shaping my work into a coherent book. I am forever grateful. Your beautiful illustrations have added a visual dimension far beyond what my stick figures could convey.

A huge debt of gratitude goes to the students of my Fall 2009 speech class, without whom this book would not exist. Their willingness to embrace a new way of learning inspired what has now become the SPEAKEASY Method™.

I am incredibly fortunate to have had several brilliant minds help make this book better in every way. Thank you to Katherine Sand, for your friendship, generosity, keen wit and invaluable suggestions. Lorna Reese, for always championing my work, your impeccable eye, and your remarkable line editing—WOW! Dave Bossert, who has been a serendipitous presence throughout my career, thank you for taking the time to read this—and for your kindness. And to Beth Zukowski, my very first reader.

A burst of love and gratitude to my mom, Phyllis Povell, for teaching me that my voice matters, empowering me to speak even when it's not easy, and showing me the importance of standing up for those whose voices have been silenced.

And lastly, thank you to my sons, Kai and Jaymin. You have taught me that screaming isn't always the best way to be heard and that powerful communication often requires subtlety and thoughtfulness. Your incredible coolness and the way you see the world never cease to amaze me. I am so proud to be your mom. I love you!

Appendix

Actioning Verbs

SCARE:	EXCITE:	PERSUADE:	SHOW:
Startle	Thrill	Convince	Demonstrate
Alarm	Arouse	Influence	Display
Frighten	Stir	Win Over	Illustrate
Terrify	Galvanize	Coax	Present
Shock	Spark	Encourage	Exhibit
Petrify	Energize	Sway	Manifest
Appall	Revitalize	Prompt	Depict
Intimidate	Fire up	Induce	Portray
Daunt	Electrify	Prevail upon	Reveal
Unnerve	Enthuse	Ingrain	Express
Disconcert	Inspire	Instill	Expose
Dismay	Delight	Prompt	Unveil
Horrify	Titillate	Urge	Betray
Astound	Ignite	Press	Flaunt
Overwhelm	Stimulate	Guide	Feature

ENGAGE: Absorb

Interact
Grip
Involve
Captivate
Interconnect
Enchant
Interrelate
Enrapture
Engross
Mesmerize
Fascinate
Entrance
Enthrall
Charm

RELATE: Understand

Connect
Link
Associate
Align
Identify
Merge
Bond
Converge
Commune
Harmonize
Sympathize
Unify
Empathize
Merge

Speeches I Recommend Listening To

Why I Love These Speeches

Here are some of my favorite speeches that break the mold and why I think they're great. They're game-changers in the world of public speaking and a testament to the power of words and the art of communication.

Michelle Obama - Democratic National Convention, 2024
Michelle Obama's 2024 DNC speech redefines public speaking in the 21st century, positioning it alongside the legendary speeches of Martin Luther King Jr. and Abraham Lincoln as one of the greatest of all time. Her words are poetry in motion, delivered with fearless warmth and a calm yet commanding presence that captures attention instantly. Her style is Shakespearean in cadence, blending rhythmic elegance with a powerful message. She weaves personal stories with broader themes of hope and resilience, transcending political divides with grace and dignity. Her ability to connect emotionally while maintaining sophistication is beyond compare.

Jane McGonigal - Gaming Can Make a Better World - TED Talk, 2010

Jane McGonigal's style is energetic and visionary, and she delivers her ideas with contagious optimism. In her first TED Talk, she presents a groundbreaking perspective on how gaming can be harnessed to solve real-world problems. McGonigal's vibrant mix of research, individual experience, and engaging storytelling is an essential must-watch for anyone who wants to speak with intelligence, humor, and a touch of humility,

Terry Moore - How to Tie Your Shoes - TED Talk, 2005

Terry Moore's talk is a perfect example of simplicity with impact. In just a few minutes, he turns an everyday task into a meaningful lesson on the importance of attention to detail. Moore's clear and approachable style demonstrates how small, thoughtful changes can significantly improve everyday life.

My Nephew Abram's Heartfelt Eulogy for Uncle Billy

The best speeches are often not recorded—the heartfelt eulogy, the memorable wedding toast, or the impassioned plea at a city council meeting. These moments are the real deal. If you hear a speech that sticks with you, ask for a copy, study the ones you love, and listen closely. There's a lot to learn from these unpolished gems.

Recommended Books to Explore

Why I love these resources

Exploring these must-reads—which have inspired and guided me on my way to getting better at this stuff—is a great way to dive deeper into the world of public speaking and communication.

Actions: The Actors' Thesaurus by Marina Caldarone
A fantastic resource for actioning, offering a rich vocabulary of action verbs to help bring performances to life.

Practice Perfect by Doug Lemov
Learn how deliberate practice can transform your skills with actionable insights that apply to public speaking and beyond.

If I Understood You, Would I Have This Look on My Face?: My Adventures in the Art and Science of Relating and Communicating by Alan Alda
Alda's book is accessible and brilliant. It explores the nuances of effective communication by blending science and storytelling.

The Emotion Thesaurus: A Writer's Guide to Character Expression, 2nd Edition by Becca Puglisi and Angela Ackerman
An invaluable tool for adding depth and authentically conveying a range of emotions to your audience.

In the Blink of an Eye: A Perspective on Film Editing, 2nd Edition by Walter Murch and Francis Ford Coppola
Explore the art and philosophy of film editing with lessons that translate beautifully to the timing and pacing of public speaking.

Acting: The Gister Method by Joe Alberti
Discover a unique approach that emphasizes emotional truth and connection, enhancing your ability to engage an audience.

The Film Director's Intuition: Script Analysis and Rehearsal Techniques by Judith Weston and Dreamscape Media
Gain insight into the director's craft with techniques that can help you analyze and prepare your presentations more effectively.

Infectious Generosity: The Ultimate Idea Worth Spreading by Chris Anderson
Learn from the curator of TED Talks himself as he shares what makes ideas powerful and worth spreading.

Freeing the Natural Voice by Kristin Linklater
Unlock the power of your natural voice with this transformative guide, offering exercises and insights to enhance vocal clarity, expression, and presence.

***Navigating Communication with Seriously Ill Patients,
2nd Edition*** by Robert M Arnold, Anthony L Back, Elise C
Carey, James A Tulsky, Gordon J Wood, and Holly B Yang
Although essential for serious illness, this book is not just
for medical professionals. It is an invaluable guide for anyone looking to enhance their communication skills with
compassion and empathy, stressing the importance of
taking time when communicating.

And of Course . . .

Mad Libs by Leonard Stern and Roger Price

The Actor's Nightmare by Christopher Durang

About Tonia Jenny

Tonia Jenny is an editor, designer, author and illustrator on a mission to bring more awareness to the benefits of a "life by hand." She believes that art, beauty and creativity are expressions of our souls and that things made by *humans* matter.

She has supported creative types in publishing their messages of inspiration for 20 years and loves nothing more than helping others awaken to the beauty that exists within. Tonia gets an impressive amount of joy taking part in bringing more art and creative expression into a world that desperately needs it.

Follow Tonia on social media and visit her website to learn more about how she can help you publish your own book.

 @toniajenny
 @toniajennypublishing
toniajenny.com
tonia@toniajenny.com

About Lynn Aliya

Lynn Aliya is a public speaking coach and consultant specializing in medical empathy. She trains doctors in empathetic communication and helps them navigate difficult conversations with greater compassion.

She is also an award-winning actor, playwright and director with thirty years in the entertainment industry. Lynn created and hosted the hit television show "The Buzz on 82."

Lynn—a.k.a. Brooklyn—is a country radio broadcaster who lives in a small town outside of Aspen. She splits her time between Colorado and New York City and is the proud mom of two incredible sons.

🌐 speakeasymethod.net.

Barrow Street

SPEAKEASY: A Radically New Approach to Public Speaking by Lynn Aliya

Unlock the secrets to dynamic public speaking with SPEAKEASY, a revolutionary method designed to transform your approach and increase your confidence.

SPEAKEASY: The Easy Method: Your Essential Guide to Effortless Communication by Lynn Aliya

Simplify your public speaking journey with The Easy Method, offering straightforward techniques to enhance your delivery and engage any audience.

Discover the SPEAKEASY Method™
Transform your public speaking skills with our comprehensive courses. Visit speakeasymethod.net to explore more.